Uplifting Affirmations for Black Men to Inspire, Motivate and Empower

A Book Written for the Black Man Who Wants to Overcome Struggle and Attract Success Through Positive Words

TABLE OF CONTENTS

TABLE OF CONTENTS   2

The Power of Positive Affirmations   5

    The human's inherent need to be "adequate"...   6

    How do humans naturally react in the face of obstacles?   7

    The Fundamentals of Positive Affirmations   8

    Positive affirmation works magic, but science explains it all...   9

Making Your Affirmations a Reality – A Step by Step Guide   11

    STEP 1: PAUSE, BREAK, AND LOOK CLOSELY AT YOUR LIFE   11

    STEP 2: PRIORITIZE AS YOU GO   13

    STEP 3: BRING THE AFFIRMATIONS OUT OF THE BOX   14

    STEP 4: Speak, Act, Repeat   15

    STEP 5: Do it with the right attitude   16

Gear Up for Challenges - Preparedness Is Key   18

    PITFALL 1: TUG OF WAR BETWEEN THE CONSCIOUS AND SUBCONSCIOUS MIND   18

    PITFALL 2: SO LITTLE OF THE POSITIVE, A WHOLE LOT OF NEGATIVES   20

PITFALL 3: SINCERITY AND CONVICTION ARE MISSING 21

PITFALL 4: TRYING TO DO EVERYTHING ALL AT ONCE 22

PITFALL 5: ZERO EFFORT, LACKING DIRECTION 23

Inspiring Stories – Revisited 25

The First Black Man who Ran Home 26

The Man Who Sings Wonders 31

The Man Who Caged the Crow 36

The Man Who Reinvented Sheets 41

The Man Who Saw the World Beyond Lenses 46

150 AFFIRMATIONS FOR SELF-ACCEPTANCE, SELF-ESTEEM, AND SELF-LOVE 51

200 POSITIVE AFFIRMATIONS FOR A SUCCESSFUL CAREER 66

150 POSITIVE AFFIRMATIONS FOR HAPPINESS 81

150 AFFIRMATIONS FOR LOVE AND RELATIONSHIPS 93

100 Affirmations for Health and Wellness 104

100 AFFIRMATIONS FOR INVESTMENTS, BUSINESS, AND FINANCIAL SUCCESS 111

50 AFFIRMATIONS FOR CREATIVITY 119

50 Affirmations for Academic Success 123

50 Affirmations for Spiritual Awakening, Alignment, and Growth 128

75 Affirmations for Healing the Soul, Mind, and Body   132

200 AFFIRMATIONS FOR STRESS MANAGEMENT, ANXIETY, AND DEPRESSION   138

The Power of Positive Affirmations

One of the major breakout stars of the 21st century is positive affirmations, more popularly known as "manifestations." Success stories and testimonies from all kinds of people circled on the internet, encouraging others to dive into the recently found power...

And the thing is, positive affirmations have been existing in our lives for so long. You may have even used it in the past, and you just didn't know. In fact, there are probably hundreds, if not thousands, of self-help books forged from tenets of self-affirmation.

Psychologists and scientists from every corner of the world were intrigued as they did astound myriads of case studies and experiments investigating the impacts of positive affirmations on a person's thought process, behavior, and, most importantly, quality of life.

The clamor around self-affirmation is enough to draw anyone in. But the very first thing this book will teach you is to never dive into unknown waters. Remember, no one can ever harness the power and use its full potential without knowing what it is and what it does.

> **DID YOU KNOW THAT:**
> Many successful men of color practice positive affirmations. Amongst them are Denzel Washington and Will Smith.

The human's inherent need to be "adequate"...

Humans are born with an intrinsic need to seek, establish, and maintain a positive image or idea of themselves. It is in our very nature to pursue paths and decisions that give us a sense of personal adequacy, more so competence. Psychologists coined this state as "self-integrity."

But if it is so "natural" for us, why are we still struggling? Why do we feel so unsure of ourselves? Why do we think so little of our abilities? Why does this book exist? Why are you flipping through its pages as if you were looking for a quick fix?

The answer is very simple - the world.

It's never easy to paint beautiful pictures of us, especially when the universe seems to be telling you the opposite. Truth be told, the world is a giant bully. It bruises you, scars you, and pounds your self-integrity to the ground.

And I couldn't think of a better example than racism. For the longest time, people of color have been subjects of human rights violations, social injustices, and blatant discrimination just because they have a darker skin color than the rest of the world. Such an environment knocks out the fundamental drive of a person to seek and nurture personal adequacy.

Social constructs, stereotypes, norms, tradition, culture, social class, and education are just some of the things that diminish the way we see ourselves.

But thankfully, the human race has been wired to survive, adapt, and then thrive. During the most vulnerable times, we humans learn to rise above challenges and succeed.

How do humans naturally react in the face of obstacles?

Every day, you can encounter several circumstances that often challenge your self-worth. These threats can range from as simple as being late for work or as big as flunking an interview.

According to psychologists, people under stressful situations react by directing their full attention to the looming threat. For example, you are about to go to a job interview. Naturally, you'll feel anxious, stressed, and nervous. Even before finishing the appointment, negative thoughts flood your mind, such as the possibility of failure.

At this point, the mind retaliates by turning on your defensive mechanisms. And these mechanisms vary from person to person. While some are good, some mechanisms can also be detrimental to your psychological well-being (i.e., avoidance, denial, and projection).

The Fundamentals of Positive Affirmations

Recognizing the fact that not all our supposed "built-in defenders" do us good in the face of threats, psychologists designed strategies called "interventions" to modify thoughts, behavior, and feelings. One of the most successful and

> **TRIVIA:**
>
> Recent studies suggest that positive affirmations activate the known pleasure centers of the brain. These are the same regions that respond to other pleasurable activities such as satiety and awards.

critically-acclaimed forms of psychological intervention is positive affirmation. You may probably know it as the "I (or I can) statements" that manifest a goal, a feeling, or a reality.

The first thing to understand about positive affirmation is that it is a practice. Some would even say that it is a way of life because only through consistency and repetition that one can achieve the best results.

Positive affirmation banks on the concept of self-integrity and personal worth. By constantly feeding your mind with positive thoughts and desired reality, you will be able to preserve the personal image you created for yourself and then follow the remarkable changes and improvements you want to see in your life.

Positive affirmation works magic, but science explains it all...

Positive affirmation is not some sort of alchemy or witchery. Its popularity is strongly backed up by credible science that attests to its long-term benefits for an individual.

In the previous subsection, the book discussed the usual ways people under stress react. They just simply focus on the threat and activate their defense mechanisms. However, the story is completely different for self-affirmed individuals.

Studies reveal that people who practice affirmation significantly widen their perspectives that they can treat psychological threats as parts of a bigger picture. They also become quite resistant to the simple stressors they encounter in their day-to-day lives.

Professionals explain that the effects of positive affirmation work in two major ways. It lessens the impact of threats as well as prevents the onset of unhealthy defensiveness.

Positive affirmation fosters a healthy and approach-oriented action towards a challenge. Instead of avoiding and denying the existence of a problem, self-affirmation equips a person with the best behavior, appropriate mindset, as well as motivation to confront and address the threats without feeling small and unworthy.

Take Away:

Positive affirmation strengthens your confidence in your own values and abilities. It constantly reassures you that you can, and you will, even in the face of great adversities.

Making Your Affirmations a Reality – A Step by Step Guide

In life, nothing ever comes easy. No one can ever achieve something without putting in some work. And as your partner in this journey, this book prepared a comprehensive and effective mix of strategies, tips, and blueprints to make your affirmations your reality.

STEP 1: PAUSE, BREAK, AND LOOK CLOSELY AT YOUR LIFE

Try to remember the last time you sat in silence just to look at your life. The chances are you seldom do it. You are probably so caught up in life that you rarely evaluate yourself, your relationships, motivations, and life in general. So, your first project will be to know yourself and your life.

Make some time for retrospection. Select a conducive environment where you can think well and feel comfortable. Then, take a careful look at every aspect of your life – relationships, career, personal goals, and experiences. While you do this, also try to identify your strengths and weaknesses.

True enough, confronting your life head-on is extremely difficult. It would require mental fortitude as well as emotional preparedness. But this is necessary for positive affirmation to work.

Here are some helpful prompts you can use in your journey of knowing yourself:

- How do I feel about myself?
- In general, how would I describe my life in one word?
- What are my goals for the future?
- What are the biggest challenges I faced in the past?
- How did I overcome those challenges?
- What are my greatest fears?
- How is my relationship with my family? Friends? Loved ones?
- What am I most proud of in my life?
- What is the most regrettable moment in my life?
- What is my best quality?
- What is my worst quality?
- What are the major factors influencing my impression of myself?
- How do I usually react to criticisms?
- What do I like to improve in myself?
- What do I like to achieve in life?
- How am I in a relationship?
- What do I do when things go wrong?
- Are my reactions toxic or healthy?

- What did I dislike in my previous relationships?
- What stressors can disrupt my mood?
- How am I as a leader? As a subordinate?
- How do I feel about my job?
- What are my long-term goals?
- What stops me from pursuing my passion?
- Am I happy with my life?
- Who do I care for the most?
- Why do I feel detached from some things in life?

STEP 2: PRIORITIZE AS YOU GO

> **TIP FROM THE AUTHOR:**
>
> Look at the mirror and think about the life you live. Ask yourself the most pressing questions. It is in these questions you discover what you desire the most.

This book highly recommends that you make a list of things or aspects of your life that you want to achieve or improve—the more specific, the better. You can dedicate a journal where you can write about your emotions and thoughts on the process.

And as you jot down your goals, rank them based on priority. Ask yourself: "What do I value the most?" The highest-priority goal is a good way to start, although there are some people who can work on multiple goals simultaneously.

STEP 3: BRING THE AFFIRMATIONS OUT OF THE BOX

Now that you have your eyes set on the goal, the next thing to do is to prepare your positive affirmations. This book packs hundreds of positive affirmations for every aspect of life. You are free to choose the statement that best suits your aspirations as well as your personality.

For example, you're a fresh graduate looking for your first job; you can pick up the following affirmations (page X):

> "I am smart and capable."
>
> "I am who I believe I am."
>
> "I am happy with myself."

But you are not restricted to constructing your own affirmations. However, you must familiarize yourself with the requirements because the syntax and semantics of positive affirmations can influence you.

Tips on Writing Positive Affirmations:

- Stick to the right verb tense. Be in the present.
- "I" is power. Always put yourself in the statement.
- Don't beat around the bush. Be specific and straightforward.

- Write in a positive tone. Never use "I am not, I don't, I cannot, etc."
- Inject an emotion into the statement.
- Make it believable and achievable.
- Write a statement that sticks.
- Keep it short and easy to remember.
- Transform your bad qualities into positive statements.

    Example: "I often make mistakes because I'm careless." -> "I am meticulous. I can make this right."

- Use strong and actionable verbs.

STEP 4: Speak, Act, Repeat

"Success isn't always about greatness. It's about consistency. Consistent hard work leads to success. Greatness will come." – Dwayne Johnson.

The heart of this guide lies in practice. Positive affirmations are statements that need to be recited several times before they take effect.

The most widely used practice of affirmation is what this book calls the "ritual." Start and end your day by standing in front of the mirror. Look yourself in the eye. Say the positive affirmations out loud and with conviction. Repeat more than 3 times. Keep your ears open while you speak. Listen attentively. Imbibe each word and believe that its' true and possible.

The book's second major lesson (as mentioned before) is that affirmation is a practice and a way of life. This only means that techniques like the ritual must be repeated A LOT OF TIMES to be effective.

Lastly, always remember that consistency is the key. Make it a perfect routine and never miss a day.

STEP 5: Do it with the right attitude

Anything that you do that lacks heart and determination can never succeed.

The ultimate secret behind the success of positive affirmation is the right mix of attitudes. If you do it just because, the results will certainly be less than what is expected.

The first pointer in this playbook is patience. You must accept the fact that the path towards change or your aspirations will not be quick and easy. Always remember that every good thing takes time. Trust the process and be present in the moment.

Next to patience is dedication because living with affirmations requires commitment and constant effort. You must stick to the ritual while investing real work in your goals to achieve results. And these things will be extra difficult without your heart in them.

Last but not least, pack some confidence. Be sure to celebrate your milestones, no matter how small or big they are. The moment you decide to empower yourself is already a step closer to greatness. So, hold your head high and power through!

> **MAJOR TAKEAWAY:**
>
> "Patience, determination, and confidence are the secret ingredients of success."

Gear Up for Challenges - Preparedness Is Key

The most common misconception about positive affirmation is that it works well for everybody and that it can solve everything. If this were true, the world must be easy. Unfortunately, like any procedure, the practice of positive affirmation may or may not work.

Do not be disheartened yet if you ever feel that your affirmations are not really working for you. It's just a wall and not the end.

In reality, circumstances will put your affirmations to the test - be it timing, attitude, or an external event. Nonetheless, the moment you become aware of such pitfalls will be the turning point of your journey. It will help you adjust your affirmation that it aligns well with your mentality, character, and goals.

PITFALL 1: TUG OF WAR BETWEEN THE CONSCIOUS AND SUBCONSCIOUS MIND

This problem is often experienced by people who have low self-esteem. A study conducted by psychologist James Wood revealed that repetitive declarations of positive affirmation seem to be ineffective, more so, harmful to individuals who are built or conditioned to think negatively.

> **POINT TO PONDER:**
> "The path towards success does not come without its challenges."

What happens is that positive affirmations trigger some kind of internal conflict between your conscious and subconscious mind.

For example, an average college student who was conditioned to believe he isn't intellectually gifted picked up the affirmation: "I am smart." He noticed that whenever he declared his affirmation, he was doubtful. A tiny voice inside his head seemed to be telling him otherwise. This is exactly what Pitfall 1 is – a tug of war between the conscious and subconscious mind.

And when an inner war breaks out, negative energy builds up. Your body is then forced to rely on defensive mechanisms to protect you from self-destructing. These mechanisms include a total shutdown from external stimuli such as psychological interventions that disable you from manifesting your positive affirmations.

But there are simple ways to get around this problem. First, you can re-structure your affirmations. In the case of the college student, instead of saying that he is smart, he can use the affirmation: "I am working hard to improve my cognitive abilities." This statement can be easily construed as true by the conscious mind.

Another thing you can do is convert negative thoughts into questions. Ask yourself. For example, "Am I not smart? What went wrong in my exams?" These types of questions will help you reflect and acknowledge your negative thoughts. Moreover, these questions will help your subconscious mind to respond with your affirmations garnering better results.

PITFALL 2: SO LITTLE OF THE POSITIVE, A WHOLE LOT OF NEGATIVES

Sticking to a routine is commendable, but it will never achieve good results if you don't live by its principle all day long. You are demonstrating pitfall 2 if you declare your affirmation every time you wake up and sleep but constantly think of the negatives in between. This is not really the affirmations' problem but yours.

> **TIP FROM THE AUTHOR**
> Live by the words you repeat. They should never become empty promises. Make them your truths.

Don't be mistaken, though. Being negative from time to time is acceptable. Rewiring how the brain thinks is not something that can happen overnight. However, if you rely on this and become so submissive, nothing will really happen for you.

One thing you can do to solve this is to direct your focus onto something else. Every time negative thoughts plague your mind, try to do something else. Distract yourself.

Second, try discussing your negative thoughts with a friend, family, or a professional. You can also write these thoughts in your journal. In this way, you can express and dissect the thoughts that seem to drag you down.

Last but not least is acceptance. You can include it in your daily affirmations, such as the ff:

"The world is imperfect, and so am I. BUT, I am perfectly okay with it."

"I have nothing to be afraid of my negativity. I have the power to overcome it."

"I am working towards the path of self-acceptance."

"Every day can either be good or bad. It is up to me how to react. And today, I choose to react positively."

"I have been through some worst days. I can get over this one too."

PITFALL 3: SINCERITY AND CONVICTION ARE MISSING

Always remember that effectiveness of positive affirmation is in a tight knot with your feelings and beliefs. Your declarations will definitely mean nothing if you lack the sincerity and conviction for it.

Take, for example, a person who's practicing affirmations to get into a company he does not like. What's the use of saying, "I will be hired for a job at Company X." You can say this a million times, but if your heart is not in this, the affirmation cannot really help you manifest this goal.

Conviction is also a vital element for positive affirmations to work. The first person that needs to believe in you is you. Believe that you can and you will. And imbibe such belief whenever you declare your affirmations. Not everyone knows this, but the way you say the affirmations has power. They only become your reality once you start believing that they are.

PITFALL 4: TRYING TO DO EVERYTHING ALL AT ONCE

People tend to overcompensate in the quest for perfection. And as ideal as "perfect" sounds, it actually has negative effects on you.

Physically, you'll feel tired and lethargic. You carry so much burden that no one really asked you to. But the heavier toll is on your mental health. You are constantly pressured to be the best, to be more. Pressure and fatigue are definitely not the best of friends. But when combined, they can crush your will and passion for living.

This deadly duo is what pitfall 4 talks about. It's good that you are aware of your goals and points for improvement. But people who strive for perfectionism always go way beyond that; they lose sight of the actual goal. They always expect more that they forget self-acceptance. They often compare themselves to others, and they forget to appreciate their own victories. And this is not the way to live with positive affirmations.

While it can be difficult to acknowledge one's perfectionism, self-evaluation is the best way to overcome this pitfall. Talk to yourself. Ask your how's and why's. These prompts can help you get through this:

1. Do I make things seem worse even though they are not?
2. How do I put pressure on myself?
3. How is it affecting my life in the present?
4. How do I handle the pressure?
5. Do I really need to be the best?
6. How would this affect my future?
7. Is this the worst that could happen, or am I just making it out to be such?

PITFALL 5: ZERO EFFORT, LACKING DIRECTION

Positive affirmations are not some kind of incantations or magic words that will make your dreams come true. The master of your fate is you. No one can do it other than you. People who fail to understand this are doomed to fail.

To achieve a goal, one must have a plan, and it must highlight the steps necessary to reach the goal. It's like a road map that can keep your focus and direction on point.

This is one of the most common mistakes committed by people. They dive head-on without having an idea of how to get there. And the more you get lost, the more hopeless you become, thus diminishing the original drive you had before starting your journey.

Having a plan is step one. The rest is putting it to action. Invest some efforts to get results in return. Positive affirmations help the process to go smoothly, but they will not make something happen for you.

A college student sticks to an affirmation: "I can score an A+ on my Calculus test." He does the ritual consistently. However, he does not spend substantial time studying the subject. He went to the test completely unprepared in the belief that the affirmations stimulate certain regions of his mind that can answer the test. In the end, he failed the test and concluded that positive affirmations do not work.

Without actions, affirmations are just empty words.

MAJOR TAKEAWAY:

Perfect is ideal, but it does not exist. Life has meaning because it is beautifully imperfect. So, stop wasting your energy In trying to do the impossible. What you can do instead is to become the best version of yourself.

Inspiring Stories – Revisited

"Sometimes reality is too complex. Stories give it form."

Jean Luc Godard

The First Black Man who Ran Home

Sometime in 1919, a black boy born in Cairo, Georgia, did not know at the time the challenges waiting for him outside his mother's womb.

Even before learning how to walk, the boy's father left him, his four brothers, and his mother in poverty. Having nothing to their name, the lonely family moved to a city called Pasadena.

With five mouths to feed, his mother took several jobs to support them. Nothing seemed easy for the family, especially for a boy who's barely learning how to speak. The first challenge the world pitched to the boy was poverty.

Cashless and oftentimes hungry, the boy did not stop dreaming. He took a special interest in athletics. He began to showcase his immense talents when he was in high school. He tried out in basketball, baseball, football, and track. With sheer determination and passion, he excelled in these four sports altogether.

By the time he entered college, he knew what he wanted to do – to be in the playfield, to play ball. A long shot, he recalled. But he continued pursuing the "dream." Among his first steps was accepting a job as an athletic administrator after he left college.

After some time, he finally decided to tackle his fate. He tried out for semi-professional football leagues in some parts of California and Hawaii. He was accepted and played for two years until the US Army took him in.

Although he had never seen combat, a bigger war was waiting for him beyond the camp – racism. The boy, now a young man, is at the face of his second predicament to greatness. He was not new to this inhumane treatment, but the enormity of the problem hit him harder in the face now that he was a man in pursuit of his dreams.

He could not make peace with the world that saw him and his people differently because of their skin color. He could not make peace with the segregation, discrimination, and inequality he had to live with. He could not make peace with the fact that the only thing standing between him and his dream was his color.

Anger, frustration, and helplessness filled the young man's heart. Until one afternoon, all these negative feelings erupted in a heated argument with a bus driver.

During this time, America was enforcing strict segregation rules forcing people of color to sit at the back of public vehicles. Consequently, the young man was court-martialed. His superiors at the time, together with some of his colleagues in the army, even conspired to file false charges against him. He was crushed by the unfair treatment, betrayal, and discrimination hovering at him. He was acquitted and transferred to another camp until he was discharged honorably by the US Army.

Traumatizing as his experiences were, those did not stop him. He went back to his old football club, tried out again for several sports, and even worked as a coach for a basketball team. Until he got into the Negro professional baseball league. He was not content with this. In fact, he was dissatisfied with his performance. Looking back, he said, "I know I can do better at the time." He knew he was still a work in progress.

Even as a child, he knew perfectly what his dream was, so the next big step he took was to try out for a major league baseball team where no black man had ever played before. Courageous as he was, the try-out did not turn out to be a great story. Again and again, he was slapped with racial slurs. He was unfairly judged because he was black. Disappointed, humiliated, and tormented, the young man went home, packing up his dreams and talents.

One night in the comfort of his home, he had a thought. "Is this worth it? All that I have been through. Are they worth it? Am I? Are my dreams worth it?" Giving up could have been the easy option. But he chose to believe in himself. He chose to trust what he could do. He chose to never stop trying. And that night, he overcame his life's biggest challenge – himself.

An ordinary person could have chosen to relinquish his dreams, but the young man did not. He chose to stand by his beliefs, by himself.

And then, a huge opportunity presented itself to the young man. He was offered a chance to play in professional baseball's major league. It was truly a leap of faith.

Of course, the baseball fans in America were taken aback - a black man playing a white man's sport. He faced numerous insults and unfair calls from his peers, the audience, umpires, and even journalists. Worst was that he became a frequent target of rough plays, threats, and dehumanizing derisions. It was a long, tedious, and soul-crushing journey. But he did not let any of these get him.

He never once used any form of violence to answer back. He remained intact and composed. He always said, "I know myself more than they know me. I am stronger and better than them all combined."

People around him started seeing him for who he truly was – a man of honor. His team came to his aid whenever the young man was grilled with racial epithets. The young man slowly opened himself up to other people. It used to be him, his mother, and his wife against the world. But then, he learned slowly that he, too, could have new friends who got his back.

It did not take long before he made a name for himself. His athletic prowess, unbreakable character, and ironclad determination struck his teammates, his opponents, the audience, and the world. He became an inspiration to children, both black and white, to pursue their dreams, no matter how unfavorable their circumstances were. His life is a testament that good things happen to those who believe in themselves.

The number on his back was 42. And yes, the young man was the great Jackie Robinsons of the Brooklyn Dodgers.

"A life is not important except in the impact it has on other lives."

Jackie Robinson

The Man Who Sings Wonders

How can someone who never saw the light know more about the world? How can someone who can't look at people's eyes understand humanity more? How can someone who was born in darkness perceive love better than most of us?

The universe seemingly denied a young boy the chance to see the moment he was born. But in exchange, he was given superb talents in music. The boy showcased promising performances at an early age while playing several instruments like piano, harmonica, and drums. He even produced a studio-recorded album at the age of 12. A great feat, many would say.

The blind kid continued paving his musical career. At 13, he was already the youngest artist to top the Billboard Hot 100. But it wasn't all rainbows with his life. Alongside puberty were his changing vocals that challenged his musical career. Some of his songs never made it to the charts. Some were never noticed and, worse, forgotten.

But the young man was not disheartened. Soon, he found artists who shared the same musical passion he had, which further honed his natural talents. Together, they composed songs that would later become great hits.

Until an unfortunate event happened in his 20s that totally changed how he looked at life. While he was on his way to a benefit concert, the young man got into a horrible car accident. He was badly injured. He was in a coma for four straight days. After waking up, he discovered that he had temporarily lost his sense of smell and taste.

It would be impossible to describe the dejection and trauma the young man went through. Any man who was born blind and on the verge of losing two other senses would be downright hopeless and depressed. But the young man never lost hope. He knew he was destined for something greater.

Determined and willful, the young man decided to undergo rehabilitation to regain his senses, and he succeeded. Aside from his senses of taste and smell, the young man also gained a new perspective on life. He often described the experience as "life-changing."

First, he discovered a deeper sense of spirituality. His life-threatening experience made him appreciate more of his existence in the universe that he was born to fulfill a purpose bigger than himself. Each time he recalled the experience, he was always filled with gratitude. If not for that experience, he could have remained in the bubble that secluded him from the pleas of the world.

But the most important thing he gained from the accident was love. Being popular at an early age, the young man lost track of his true self. He was busy composing songs that he forgot that there were people who loved him for who he truly was, not just the boy wonder they heard sing.

In his own words, the young man said, "It was at that moment when I felt truly loved. Not as a musical prodigy but as a real person."

With all the fame and success he had under his belt, the young man continued to become an inspiration to many people around the globe. His disability never became an obstacle in creating music that was loved by many. Even more so, he used his music and influence to raise awareness on very important societal issues such as equality and human rights.

One of his beacons was Martin Luther King Jr., a prominent civil rights movement leader during the 1950s. He was a teenage boy when he first met Martin Luther. His life was changed forever. He came to understand the depth and reach of inequality and what it did to children, their families, and to their future. He knew and related so well to the feeling of deprivation.

When Martin Luther King Jr. was assassinated, the young boy paid his respects and joined a cause asking the US government to commemorate the contributions of Luther King Jr. to democracy. He even set aside his musical career to participate in rallies to convince the US congress. The signature of the late US Pres. Ronald Raegan, on the bill mandating the civil rights activist's birthday as a national holiday, was one of his biggest joys.

If someone were to look at the young man's life, it would be obvious that the biggest influence of Martin Luther King

Jr. in his life could be seen through his humanitarian projects. He made his music as an instrument to help and support others. He organized fund-raising concerts for victims of calamity, diseases, and abuse. Some of the charities he supported addressed poverty, hunger, AIDS, gender equality, disaster relief, environment, and substance abuse.

He became an icon that channeled not only his financial resources but also his passion and talents to causes greater than himself. He made something more special out of the amazing voice he was given. He used it to raise awareness, reinvigorate volunteerism, and help create a more inclusive world. More than his greatest hits, he will be remembered as a human rights hero.

It is amazing how a young boy deprived of sight saw more of the world than people who have perfectly good eyes. Not only did he see, but he felt and empathized with the suffering of people.

Stevie could have been a regular person, but he decided to become more, to make something mean more. He refused to be defined and limited by what others call "disability." He was incomplete, but he lived completely. He knew he was born strong and that he could overcome the biggest challenges life threw at him. But he did not stop there. He extended his power to help others. He used his own life to inspire and empower others.

Just like his famous lyrics,

"Don't let anybody take you to a low level.

Just keep on and keep on until you reach higher ground..." Little Stevie is encouraging you to be yourself, to love yourself, and to share that love with others.

"We all have the ability. The difference is how we use it."

— Stevie Wonder

The Man Who Caged the Crow

A man of color living in the present stepped into a wormhole and was transported back to the past, sometime in the 1870s. Disoriented as he was, he began walking along the alleys of America. He tried to approach a white man he met to ask questions. But to his surprise, the man, as well the people who saw him, berated him.

When the white men finally left him alone, an African American came to his rescue. The good man asked him, "What in the world were you trying to do? Did you forget the law?" The modern man was so confused. He asked, "How am I at fault?"

The good man answered back, "You know that white and black are not supposed to be equals. We have laws preventing us from interacting directly. Where are you from, really?" The modern man felt aghast by how different the world was at the time. And then he began telling the good man his story, what the future is like, and how it came to be like that.

He began his story in a small district in Washington D.C. called Striver's section. A middle-class family from the descendant of former slaves gave birth to an outstandingly courageous boy who would soon change the world for the better.

The young boy's father was a son of a former slave. But even so, his father worked hard to become a lawyer. Following in his father's footsteps, the talented young man showed a promising academic performance since he was a child. He graduated valedictorian of his class and was awarded by a renowned honor society.

And when World War I erupted, the young man's fate took a drastic turn. He decided to join the ranks of the US Army. Instead of camaraderie and brotherhood, he personally witnessed and experienced the worst of racial segregation while in the army.

The man felt frustrated and furious at the system that fueled hate, discrimination, and injustice. He found it laughable and beyond crazy to die defending a flag that does not treat him and his peers equally. So he promised himself, "I made up my mind that if I got through this war, I would study law and use my time fighting for men who could not strike back."

And with a stroke of fate, the young man went home alive after the war. With a newfound purpose, the man applied and got accepted into a prestigious university where he studied law. He stayed true to his promise. After he graduated, he practiced law while mentoring young generations of black lawyers. Some of his mentees were able to take a seat in the state's highest court.

After all that he did as an educator and a mentor, he knew that a lot of things had still to be done for his people. So, he decided to face the problems outside the university. He became a forefront defender of black people's rights.

One of the biggest battles he faced was the one with the Crows. Jim Crow was notorious for tormenting colored people. He treated people with colored skin inhumanely and unfairly. Under his powers, no black man was ever allowed to directly interact with a white person. Any black man or woman who was found disobeying the racial segregation laws was punished and, worse, shamed.

Together with his peers, the man got tired of living in such a rotten world. "It's time we take a step forward," they said. Talented as he was, the man became a fearless litigator. He challenged every Crow he came across.

The first among his remarkable battles was the one against the Crow law mandating racial segregation in public schools. Not only that, but the law also violated a person's right to quality education.

The good black man knew how important and valuable education was to a person's future. So, he poured so much of his energy and powers to ensure that no black child will ever be denied the opportunity to hone their talents just because of the color of their skin.

He did not just stop at education; he tackled one Crow at a time. Next to education, he fought against the Crows endangering the lives of poor black men. He became a defender of black men being unfairly judged by an all-white jury. These men were wrongfully convicted and sentenced to death.

He could not stomach the injustice filling the courts of justice. He could not bear the sight of innocent men being killed just because of his color. No matter how difficult and unfavorable his chances were, the good man did all that he could to save their lives.

Of course, his battles were tedious, devastating, and crushing. He was not able to save them all. One of his biggest heartbreaks was when he failed to save an innocent black man from a lifetime of imprisonment. Even on his deathbed, he knew that the court's decision was baseless and unconstitutional.

He moved on, but he never forgot. He used this as his motivation to become stronger and undefeatable in court. He continued plowing the field of equality by dismantling the lies paraded by Crow laws.

He was not able to bring all of them down, but he succeeded in one thing – he empowered many talented people from both races to protect the rights of colored people.

As soon as the modern man finished his story, the African American man was crying. He told the modern man how his dreams were always a future without discrimination and segregation. Just before the modern man disappeared, the man smiled and told him, "I cannot wait for my children to live in the future where we are seen as beautiful people."

When the modern man got back to the future, he discovered that the man who helped him was the grandfather of the great Charles Hamilton Houston, the civil rights hero.

The Man Who Reinvented Sheets

It was just another day for Kevin. He got up in his bed, still feeling sleepy and unmotivated. He dragged his feet into his bathroom and started preparing for the day.

While he brushed his teeth, Kevin stared at his image in the mirror. Two questions lingered on his mind, "Do I like myself better today? What does the future hold for me?"

Kevin is a married man with kids. He knew that everything going on in his life was fine. But he constantly felt that something was missing. Kevin felt that life had been too mediocre and regular that he no longer felt excited and driven. It's like he was in constant pursuit of inspiration that could fuel his lack of creativity and motivation.

Just before he left the house, he received a call from a familiar number. The person on the other line informed him that his good friend Isaac was rushed to the hospital the previous night for his existing medical condition. Worried as he truly was, Kevin immediately decided to take the day off to pay a visit to Isaac.

When he arrived at the hospital, he hurriedly approached the information desk to ask for Isaac's room number. The nurse answered, "He is in room 304. But you might need to wait before you could meet him because the patient is still undergoing a series of tests."

Kevin headed for the coffee shop on the opposite side of the hospital. And while he walked along the busy corridors of the hospital, he came across a hospital room for sick kids. Intrigued, he peeked inside, where he looked at the kids' faces. Apart from the apparent sadness in the kids' eyes, Kevin noticed something else. He sensed the languor and longing.

These kids were supposed to be outside, playing, exploring, and having fun. "How can life be so cruel to these young kids?" Kevin thought to himself. And the truth is, Kevin was never fond of hospitals. Since he was young, hospitals had always looked grim and depressing to him. It must be unimaginable for kids who must stay there for most of their childhood.

Kevin quietly sipped his hot coffee as he waited for Isaac to return to his room and when he finally returned, the two men hugged and talked. Kevin felt relieved when Isaac explained to him what had happened. Although it would take several weeks of rest, Isaac remained safe. Their conversation seemed to be endless, but Kevin noticed the time and bade goodbye to Isaac. He promised to come back in the following days to keep him company.

As soon as Kevin arrived home, he told his wife about Isaac and the hospital. He particularly described his encounter with the kids. "Hon, I felt sad for the kids. The room was too normal... It makes the whole thing even more saddening. How can hospitals not care?" As a dad himself, he couldn't bear the idea of his own kids staying in that very same room. And that's when a brilliant idea struck Kevin's mind – bed sheets.

This idea was life-changing for Kevin. He found a new purpose, a purpose bigger than himself. And this was probably what he was looking for in the past.

He knew something inside him ignited. Creativity, drive, and other positive energies flowed naturally within him. Ideas after ideas come into his mind. He paired his creative imagination with valuable research. He read about the fun and intellectually stimulating activities for kids. He kept on thinking about how to integrate fun and learning in a one-bed sheet for kids.

True enough, the process was long and difficult. It took Kevin almost two years to develop and manufacture bedsheets for kids. He worked hard in hand with teachers and healthcare professionals regarding his project. Soon, he established his own company, which he named "Playtime Adventures."

Kevin was a good-hearted man who wanted to help sick children. But making money out of his idea is another story. No matter how good his intentions were, making sales was his major problem. He heard so many Nos before he succeeded.

It was understandable, Kevin reasoned out to himself. People always felt hesitant and doubtful about things they just saw. And more importantly, who would like to invest in interactive bed sheets. As destructive as these thoughts were, Kevin stood his ground. He knew that his idea was worth something and that it could help children, and not just the ones in the hospital.

Just like what he believed, Kevin made his first sales. He felt so proud of himself for not giving up, no matter how unfriendly the situation looked. When asked about this, Kevin always answered, "I have trust in my ideas, in my principles, and in myself. That's why I always choose to move forward and power through."

And soon, more and more people saw the value in Kevin's interactive bed sheets. It also became accessible for regular kids who wished to have fun at home. Parents, doctors, nurses, teachers, and healthcare workers acknowledged the impact Kevin brought to the lives of the children.

Kevin became a successful businessman who is known by many. But even so, he did not forget once the inspiration of where his company was founded – altruism. Helping others had been his forefront agenda. His company supported multiple charities for children. They are also quick responders in times of need. Kevin always told people that the heart of his company is the welfare of children.

Who could have thought that a successful and well-loved black man once lived in emptiness? It may seem that your days are only passing, but never lose trust in the process. Sometimes, your best ideas are just waiting for the most perfect time. And it may not only change your life but also the lives of people around you, just like Kevin.

This short story was inspired by an American entrepreneur named Kevin Gatlin.

"You will need to have a high tolerance for this because you will hear the word 'NO' every day once you start your business! I live by the saying, 'God will never put more on me than I can bear. I just have a high tolerance level for pain!'"

Kevin Gatlin

The Man Who Saw the World Beyond Lenses

"You can't make it. It's a complete waste of time and money." As young as 8 years old, Parks was told that he could not succeed in life. The world looked black and white in his perspective. Only the whites were given the right to live, while the rest of them only got what was left.

Parks was the youngest among the 15 children of an African American couple living in Kansas. Poverty and hunger were his company. To make things worse for the little boy, he was a frequent target of bullying and discrimination due to his skin color.

One afternoon, on his way home, Parks ran into three white boys. After calling him names, the white boys threw poor Parks into the river to drown. Parks held his breath for as long as he could until the three boys left. Dripping wet, Parks continued walking home. He wiped the tears that seemed to flow endlessly from his eyes. He felt small and powerless.

Life became harder for Parks. When he was 14, he came home to his mother's death. He loved her so dearly. He spent the entire night hugging his dead mother. It was his way of letting go of someone so close to his heart.

After that, he was forced to live with one of his sisters and her husband in another city. He missed his own life. It was not ideal, but at least he had a loving mother waiting for him every day.

His new life was not in any way friendly. His sister's husband did not like Parks, and he displayed his apparent hostility with the boy conspicuously. As a result, Parks ran away, and this marked the start of his life on the streets.

Parks was only 15 when he started working to provide for himself. He tried doing all jobs available to him. He worked in brothels and restaurants as a busboy. Surprisingly, the young boy had so many skills packed in his bag. He could sing and play instruments well. He was also athletic, which enabled him to play briefly as a semi-professional basketball player.

But Parks had always wanted to learn more about the world. So, when he got to a gentleman's club, he immediately grabbed the chance to educate himself. He picked up books from the club's library and learned what he could from them. No one was more disappointed than Parks when the club closed its doors due to the impending economic crisis.

With newfound determination, Parks, now a young man, hopped into a train and tried his luck in Chicago. He got a job in a flophouse where he served travelers from various regions. One of the things Parks always looked forward to in this job was when clients left picture magazines in their rooms. It was like a treasure to Parks.

He discovered the magic and wonder in photographs in those magazines. As he flipped one page to another, feelings of amazement, excitement, and curiosity swelled inside him. Among the first photographs he saw, the most memorable for him were the pictures of migrant workers in America. It struck him in ways he could never describe in words. From then on, he discovered what he wanted to do, what he dreamt of becoming.

He saved every penny he could from his jobs. One day, he came to a pawnshop and excitedly bought his first-ever camera. He knew nothing of photography, but he was determined. He taught himself one step at a time.

It was a hobby at first, something he loved doing. He did photography whenever he could, in between jobs. Like every artist, Parks took a while before he harnessed his raw talent. It also took him some time before he discovered his inspiration. And it's not something beautiful or aesthetically pleasing. Parks' inspiration was the truth.

He went back to the very reason why he fell in love with photography – the pictures of migrant workers. He aspired to tell the world the stories of people with no fame nor wealth under their names. He aspired to photograph humanity without the taints of gender, race, ethnicity, and religious beliefs. He wanted to show the truest nature of a person.

Parks had the eyes of a great photographer because he captured photos that no one could have. As soon as he got his films developed, Parks garnered recognition. A clerk working at the shop encouraged him to work for a magazine to showcase his talents.

Not long after, Parks got a job in a fashion magazine where he was noticed by more prominent persons. And his biggest break came when he was awarded a Julius Rosenwald Fellowship. Along with a hefty compensation, the fellowship offered him steady employment – something that he had always wanted.

Instead of working for star-studded companies, he decided to take pictures for the Farm Security Administration (FSA), an organization that tackled societal issues, issues that he knew so well like poverty, discrimination, and inequality.

When FSA shut down, the rising Parks began freelancing until he stumbled at Life magazine, where he became the first-ever African American photojournalist. Throughout his career in the magazine, his camera focused on social injustices experienced by real-life people in every era. No one could photograph such events better than him. He captured photos that had endless stories to tell.

But of course, he faced so many challenges along with his career as a black photographer. His peers and his audience altered his photographs and his motives often. They twisted his works as they saw fit. This was when Parks realized that his photographs were not enough. He needed exact words to tell his stories, so he began his journey as a writer.

He was able to write award-winning photo essays, books, and short stories. By the time Parks was 55, he was given a chance to direct his first film, the movie adaptation of his self-written novel.

After all the recognitions he received, Parks recalled that the best part of being a photographer was being able to see every person eye to eye as equals. Having to see their stories through and beyond the lenses of his camera was his life treasure.

Gordon Parks was not only the greatest photojournalist that lived in the 20th century, but he was also an inspiration to people struggling in life. He could have chosen to give up multiple times in his life, but he did not. He chose to believe in himself, and maybe, he convinced the world, too, that he could make it. And he did.

> "I saw that the camera could be a weapon against poverty, against racism, against all sorts of social wrongs. I knew at that point I had to have a camera."
> Gordon Parks

150 AFFIRMATIONS FOR SELF-ACCEPTANCE, SELF-ESTEEM, AND SELF-LOVE

"Talk to yourself once a day. Otherwise, you may miss meeting an excellent person in this world."
— Swami Vivekananda

1. I am born with beautiful skin color.
2. I am proud that I am a man of color.
3. I will choose myself today, tomorrow, and always.
4. I am a man of color and honor.
5. I choose to accept the color I was born with. It is always a blessing.
6. I refuse to be reduced to my color. I am so much more than my color.
7. I free myself from the shackles of discrimination. I am so much more than what the world believes.
8. I am optimistic that others will see me for me.
9. I love my color, my community, and my roots.
10. I have nothing to be afraid of just because I am black.
11. I am black, and I am brave.
12. I am confident around others. My color is and will never be a disability.
13. I am born with a purpose.
14. My color is one of my many strengths. It contributes to who I am today.
15. I know myself to the core. I have the abilities and character to bring positivity to the world.

16. I have the power to overcome prejudices and stereotypes against men of color.
17. I am so much more than what the world is telling me.
18. I love my skin color and what it brings to my life.
19. I am loved by my peers, family, and friends for who I truly am and not because of my color.
20. I embrace my strengths and my weaknesses. I accept that I am imperfect.
21. I radiate with positive energy because I appreciate my whole self.
22. Negative words are powerless over my self-acceptance and self-esteem.
23. My self-image is only up to me. No one can influence the way I see myself as a man.
24. I am worthy of acceptance, paise, and love. I refuse to believe otherwise.
25. I am proud to be black. And I deserve all the best in the world.
26. I will be kind to myself every day even when others are not.

27. I am letting go of all the destructive and discriminative words thrown at me.
28. Being a black man is my pride.
29. I fully trust my internal strength.
30. It is only I who can dictate the way I feel about myself and my life.
31. Every day, I will wake up to love myself, including the color I am blessed with.
32. My shortcomings have nothing to do with my color. I am human, and I am free to commit mistakes.
33. I am letting go of the pressures and burdens I put on myself as a man.
34. I am human, and I am allowed to show weakness.
35. I am committed to improving myself in every aspect.
36. Today is another day to show the world that men of color are capable and reliable.
37. I am a man of color, and I deserve recognition for all my merits.
38. I will free myself from the shackles of racial discrimination.

39. I am so much more than just a black man. I am a kind, smart, and lovable person.
40. I am the best version of myself. No one can do it better than me.
41. I am letting go of the negative thoughts inculcated in my mind just because I am a black man. I will only allow positivity in my life.
42. I forgive myself for thinking that I am less than what I truly am.
43. I am freeing myself from insecurities. I am one of a kind.
44. I love every inch of myself. I will bravely showcase to the world what I have to offer.
45. I will take one step at a time towards self-acceptance.
46. I feel happy and blessed to be a black man.
47. I admire myself for being a man of color.
48. I accept the truth that I still have things to improve about myself. I am a work in progress, and I am proud of it.
49. I will invest constant effort and time to become a better version of myself.
50. My soul is as beautiful as my skin.

51. I am happy and content with the way I look, think, and act.
52. Being a man of color comes with challenges, but I am stronger. I am confident that I can rise above these hurdles because I trust myself and my abilities.
53. I can offer so much goodness to the world because I am an amazing man.
54. My self-worth is determined by my values and achievements and not by my color.
55. I will continue appreciating my true self in its every form.
56. I respect my own limitations as a man. I refuse to be reduced to what I am not.
57. I woke up today, and I chose self-love.
58. Only I can define my masculinity. It will never conform to the ugly stereotypes of the world.
59. I forgive myself for underestimating what I have and what I can do.
60. I commit to becoming a better version of myself every day.
61. I am forever grateful for my body, mind, and heart.

62. I will live as my true self no matter what others say and do against me.
63. I will continue to live by my truth as a black man.
64. Regardless of what others say, I am who I am, and I'm proud of it.
65. I am born a black man, so I am going to live with it to the best of my ability.
66. I am an empowered and influential man of color. I am confident in what I can contribute to the world.
67. I acknowledge my moments of weakness. It will never diminish my value as a man.
68. I am a black man, and I am built for great things in life.
69. I am a man of color gifted with exemplary talents.
70. My masculinity is one of my many gifts. I step on it with great pride and honor.
71. I appreciate and love myself to the core. And I will live my days emanating my self-worth.
72. As a man of color, I am expected to be strong, but I also acknowledge that I am a human first. I have my

weaknesses. It is okay to be vulnerable sometimes.
73. Knowing my true self nurtures my self-confidence.
74. My self-confidence is built from hard work, determination, and motivation to be successful.
75. My self-esteem grows every day because I am surrounded by people who appreciate the real me.
76. I welcome all the good opportunities coming my way because I am deserving.
77. My thoughts and feelings are valid. I will never let the negativity of the world tell me otherwise.
78. The world will learn to respect me and my color once I start loving and respecting myself.
79. The universe gifted me with family, friends, and colleagues that know my worth as a person. I refuse to be dragged down by discrimination and prejudice.
80. I am an exceptional man of color, and I will start living my life unapologetically.

81. As soon as I wake, I feel excitement rushing through my veins. I am thrilled to create wonderful things in the world.
82. I will not be ruled by how society sees me. I know that I am worthy and I am exceptional.
83. I am determined to live with a positive mind, releasing all the negativities I was born with.
84. I refuse to be manipulated by the need to seek validation from others. The only approval that matters is mine alone.
85. Self-love is masculine.
86. I have integrity, dignity, and honor. I can overcome anything life throws at me.
87. When I look in the mirror, I like what I see. I love my skin, my color, and my physical features. I deserve to be appreciated the way I see myself.
88. Every day is a new day to discover the good things about myself.
89. I forgive myself for my past mistakes and what could have been. They are part of life.

90. I am confident that I can do anything I set my mind to.
91. My self-worth comes from within me and not from other people.
92. I value my successes more than failures.
93. My color is not a hurdle I have to overcome. It is what truly makes me special.
94. I refuse to be bothered by comparisons. I will not be defined by societal standards.
95. I am working hard to strengthen my spirits so I can succeed in life.
96. I allow myself to be appreciated and loved by people around me.
97. Today, I choose to view myself in a positive light.
98. I am a courageous person who is open to better opportunities. I will never draw back from a challenge just because the world tells me. I am a man of color, a man of pride.
99. My potential is limitless. I can be anything I want.
100. My self-esteem grows stronger every day.

101. I take pride in my efforts to know myself better.
102. My self-worth thrives whenever I express my emotions and beliefs.
103. My success is guaranteed because I persevere even in the face of discrimination, inequality, and judgment.
104. I know my worth extremely well, and I refuse to settle for things/people I do not deserve.
105. No one can do anything in the very similar way I do. I am unique and the only one in this world.
106. I am letting go of all the false judgments made against me in the past.
107. My pursuit of self-acceptance will never be hindered by my color or masculinity. I am a man who values the importance of self-acceptance and self-love.
108. I breathe in confidence, and I exhale self-doubts.
109. My contributions to the world matter.
110. Rejections, setbacks, and mistakes fuel me to become a better version of myself every day.

111. I am committed to preserving my self-worth.
112. I am flawed, and I love myself for it. I can still improve and become better.
113. I feel complete and secure myself. I do not need anyone's opinion to make me feel this way.
114. Regardless of where life brings me, I am sure that people will see me and appreciate my abilities and character.
115. I am confident in my inner strength. I can harness it to make things happen for myself.
116. I owe to myself to feel confident about my character, talents, and abilities.
117. My well-being is my top priority. I am the most important person in my life.
118. I acknowledge that my personal growth can take time. Every step I take is already an achievement.
119. I choose to love myself more and more each day.
120. Today, I celebrate my existence, my color, my abilities, and all that I am.
121. My greatest strength is my confidence.
122. I feel more and more alive as I gradually learn to accept myself,

including my strengths, weaknesses, and insecurities.
123. I woke up with a great vision in mind – a future of bravery, confidence, and freedom.
124. My confidence gives me the courage to make big leaps in life.
125. I encourage optimism in life.
126. I believe that I can attract life-changing opportunities.
127. My self-worth inspires me to pursue the things I truly want.
128. I accept with humility constructive criticisms aimed at helping me.
129. I am here, and I matter.
130. I have a meaningful existence. I have nothing to be afraid of, so I face every day with confidence.
131. I am ruled by my own mind. I reject being controlled by the expectations and views of other people.
132. I am the master of my fate. I am in full control of my emotions, thoughts, and actions.
133. I accept that I cannot undo the past. I will focus on creating a future I like.
134. I am kind, smart, and compassionate.

135. The more I accept myself, the more confident I become.
136. I believe in myself and my potential to succeed in this life.
137. I am letting go of my insecurities and emotional scars. I will focus more on my achievements, no matter how small.
138. I feel my confidence surging inside me so are my talents.
139. I am confident in the future I am creating.
140. I recognize that being a black man comes with certain challenges. It is okay because I know I can face them head-on.
141. Positive energy flows freely in my life. It provides me the confidence to express myself.
142. I have nothing to fear. I show my true self to the world.
143. My talents are deserving of recognition.
144. I have great potential, and I'll make use of it to have a good life.
145. I permit myself to showcase my skills and abilities without reservations.

146. I have a masculinity that transforms me to become a better human.
147. My confidence and self-worth amplify every day.
148. I choose to follow the path of greatness.
149. Success, love, and happiness are headed my way because I am a good person.
150. I unleash the power within to create a life that I truly deserve.
    1.

200 POSITIVE AFFIRMATIONS FOR A SUCCESSFUL CAREER

1. I am a black man who is talented and skilled. I believe that I can land a job that is perfect for who I am.
2. I will pursue a career path that makes me happy about myself.
3. I have nothing to fear in the interview. I'm eloquent, smart, and a people person.
4. I am preparing well for my upcoming job interview and examination. I know that I will do well.
5. Every day is a new chance to get closer to my dream job.
6. I will get the call today. I know I will.
7. I am a good person, and I deserve to work in an organization that sees me as equal.
8. I am not afraid of a challenging environment. I can adapt well and succeed eventually.
9. I am committed to the goals and principles of the company I am working in.
10. I am enjoying every learning opportunity in the company.
11. The panel will see my promising potential and outstanding character.
12. Great opportunities will knock on my door today.
13. Success comes to those who are patient and hardworking.
14. I am where I should be.
15. My organization knows what I can contribute to the growth of the company. So, I will continue doing my best.

16. I am in a job that values my contributions and ideas.
17. My job makes me feel like a complete person.
18. The career I am in is the one I have always dreamed of.
19. I deserve this position because I earned it.
20. In the workplace, I am me. I never try to be someone else.
21. Like my skin, I am outstanding.
22. My team loves having me around because I am full of excellent ideas.
23. My team loves my company because I radiate positive energy.
24. I practice exceptional professionalism and work ethic.
25. I am a role model in the company. I stick to my principles, and I do my job well.
26. I attract prosperity and wealth because I am hardworking.
27. Every day is a new chance to grow in my chosen profession.
28. I am the glue that connects people in the organization.
29. I stand against any form of abuse and racial discrimination. Every person deserves to be treated equally.
30. I am claiming career success because I am determined, hardworking, and talented.

31. My dream job is coming for me. I will patiently prepare myself for it
32. I have an ironclad will. I choose to embrace all the good opportunities coming my way.
33. My team acknowledges the contributions I bring to the table.
34. My team sees me as a member and not an outsider.
35. I belong to an organization whose goals and views are aligned with mine.
36. Challenges are opportunities to learn and discover. I recognize that these are vital elements for career growth.
37. My heart and ears are open to constructive criticisms. I am always open to improving myself professionally.
38. I am a reliable member of the team.
39. I always offer assistance to my team. I make sure that we work in a friendly environment.
40. I will get a job that showcases my skills, abilities, and character. I'll never settle for anything less.
41. I am confident that I can do the tasks assigned to me.
42. I am letting go of the mistakes and errors I have committed in the past.
43. I am highly capable. I can lead my team to achieve our long- and short-term goals.
44. I use my time, energy, and resources efficiently.

45. My workmates respect me because of my good character.
46. Some people can dare to tear me down, but I am strong. I can and will overcome them.
47. I own up to my mistakes and shortcomings. They made me better at doing this job.
48. I face challenges with a clear and positive mind. I know that I can solve them with my outstanding wit, dedication, and character.
49. Every challenge I encounter is an opportunity to grow. I will never shy away from obstacles.
50. My work ethic respects the existence of company rules.
51. Today, I woke up filled with energy to do my tasks perfectly.
52. I am calm, logical, and collected.
53. I will ace this job interview because I can.
54. My job completes me. I feel so much happiness and pride in being part of this organization.
55. I always deliver outstanding outputs to the organization.
56. I am passionate about my job.
57. I have the motivation and power to chase after my goals and aspirations in life.
58. My decision is based on facts. I will not be dragged by emotions and/or bias.
59. Failures are part of life. It's completely normal.
60. I am measured by the good things I brought to this company.

61. It is completely okay to rely on others for help.
62. I am black, and I am an asset to this company.
63. I can forge the path toward my career goals.
64. Great things are happening in my career.
65. The approval of others is the least of my concerns. I am more focused on producing high-quality results.
66. I am brave, and I can speak my mind out.
67. My values are the core of my existence. I refuse to do anything that is against my morality, beliefs, practice, and dreams.
68. I wake up every morning feeling happy about my job.
69. My present job helps me to grow professionally as well as financially.
70. I recognize the need to balance my career with my time for family, social life, and self-care
71. My company hears my opinions and ideas with an open mind. I am seen as an equal and not just a man of color.
72. I am determined to create a career that works best for me.
73. I am skilled, talented, and professional. I am truly an asset to the company.
74. I am grateful for all the opportunities and growth I underwent last week.
75. I am defined by my abilities.
76. I am strong, and I can overcome any hurdle that comes my way.

77. I am committed to delivering the best results.
78. I am an exceptional, reliable, and highly capable leader.
79. I can achieve the height of my dreams.
80. I trust my skills, my ideas, and my thoughts. I believe that my presence contributes to the growth of the organization.
81. I can get this job because I know I can.
82. I will ace the interview. I have nothing to fear because I worked hard for it.
83. My success takes time. I will be patient, and I will work hard.
84. I will continue to perform at my peak, even in the face of pressure.
85. I have a strong spirit, and I can endure anything that comes at me.
86. Every challenge I overcome is a step closer to greatness.
87. I embrace all my weaknesses and shortcomings. I am working hard on turning them into my strengths.
88. Opportunities will come pouring down my way.
89. I am confident, and I can speak in front of my team.
90. I will make the best decision for my career.
91. I will be steadfast in my goals. I am closing my doors to distractions.
92. I am open to criticism. I accept them, and I work hard on improving myself.

93. I allow myself to change, grow, and become the professional I always wanted.
94. I am headed on a better professional path.
95. I have good decision-making skills. I trust the facts and my guts.
96. I will always come up with a solution no matter how challenging the situation is.
97. I am here because I love and care for my profession.
98. This job helps me to grow professionally and financially.
99. I come to work with enthusiasm and satisfaction.
100. My work ethic is exceptional. I earn respect from my peers.
101. I keep my life in balance. Work is work. What's personal is kept personal.
102. I believe in my decision-making skills. They are always aimed for the greater good.
103. I dedicate my time and efforts to advancing my career.
104. I always stick to the rules of the company.
105. I trust my boss and teammates. Together we are unbeatable.
106. I am doing my best in this career. I will succeed. I believe I will succeed.
107. I am brave enough to cooperate with others in times of crisis.
108. I am an asset that any company would be lucky to have.

109. I am at peace in my job.
110. Success is in my fate. I will happily take on the journey of achieving it.
111. I have a purpose in this team, and I do it very well.
112. I am ready to pursue higher career goals.
113. I always do what I must, regardless of how difficult it might be.
114. I strongly believe that I am destined for this job.
115. My presence inspires my colleagues to perform well.
116. I am a key person in the company who shares meaningful work with the team.
117. I earn trust and respect from my peers because of my capabilities and decision-making skills.
118. I strive to make strong and amicable relationships with my colleagues and boss.
119. I am happy about the work I do and its impact on society.
120. Great projects are coming my way. With my abilities and attitude, I know I can do it.
121. I come to work with enthusiasm, passion, and creativity.
122. I am born to do this job. I can recognize and seize an opportunity that comes my way.
123. I am deserving of recognition, awards, and promotion.
124. I am focusing all my energy, hard work, and ideas on the growth of my career.

125. I am always ready to face challenges in the workplace.
126. I accept constructive criticisms well. I use them to improve myself and further my own career.
127. Whenever my team faces a problem, I am always focused on thinking of better solutions.
128. I acknowledge the risks of changing careers. But I am me, and I trust my capabilities and attitude.
129. The path toward professional success is bumpy, but I am confident that I can power through.
130. The work I do is well-appreciated by my boss, colleagues, and clients.
131. I always remain calm in the face of pressure. I make sure to function optimally until the goal is achieved.
132. My work gives me satisfaction, confidence, and self-worth.
133. My work inspires me to pursue personal growth.
134. I am natural at my job. I am born to do this.
135. This is the perfect time to change careers. I am brave enough to take the first time today.
136. I am in a very welcoming and conducive environment that nurtures my character and abilities.
137. I strive to be a better leader to my juniors. I want to inspire and motivate them.
138. I treat my dreams as a full-time job because it is a work in progress.

139. The greatest investment I can make is in myself. I am worth it.
140. I have good stress management skills. I will never be swayed by problems coming my way.
141. It is normal to feel tired and burnt out. The most important thing is to wake up the next day and start trying again.
142. My professional career is a journey, not a hurdle. I must savor and enjoy every moment of it.
143. I treat my juniors, colleagues, and boss with equal respect.
144. I will keep on trying until I succeed in my job.
145. Endless opportunities are waiting for a black man like me. I have nothing to be afraid of.
146. I make sure to utilize my time and resources wisely. I pour them into a thing that contributes to my growth as a professional.
147. I thrive in an environment that acknowledges my worth as a person and as a professional.
148. I do not need to rush things. I will focus on my present and work hard for the future.
149. I look in the mirror, and I see a fulfilled and successful man.
150. I refuse to be compared to anyone else. I believe that a career path is unique for every individual. His timeline does not have to be mine.
151. I always discover new sides of myself as I continue on this career path.

152. I am putting my mistakes behind me. Every day is a new day to become a better employee.
153. I accept the fact that I can miss good ideas sometimes. This is why I keep my ears and eyes open for suggestions and constructive criticisms from my peers.
154. I value accuracy over speed. I prefer to have correct than speedy results.
155. I make sure to take proper rest because success does not come to sickly individuals.
156. I build my career with my own strength, moral compass, and mental fortitude.
157. It is okay to face some bumps and walls along the way. My success is not a straight path. I can make a lot of turns to achieve my triumph.
158. It is only I who can decide on my dreams.
159. My job allows me to express my creativity and innovativeness.
160. My bad moments at work will be replaced by better ones. I will keep remembering my achievements rather than my failures.
161. I refuse to be stopped by negative judgments and prejudice against my color. I deserve to be respected in the workplace.
162. With my expertise and experience, I know I can make decisions that will favor the company, my team, and our clients.
163. I always strive for the best results. No one said it was going to be easy.

164. My company compensates me generously.
165. I can create a balance among all the aspects of my life.
166. I am always yes! Yes to change, yes to new opportunities, and yes to success!
167. My dreams can become my reality through hard work and determination.
168. All victories started with a small leap, so I am having a leap of faith today.
169. I unceasingly chase knowledge and improvement.
170. I celebrate every little success I make in the office.
171. I am releasing myself from the expectations of others of me. All that matters is my opinion of myself.
172. I allow myself to chase bigger things in my career, like a big promotion.
173. I set reasonable boundaries in the workplace to protect my peace
174. I make decisions based on facts.
175. I aspire to be the kind of leader that my team needs the most.
176. I have the mind to make real-time solutions for real-life problems.
177. I always imbue my values into the work I am doing.
178. No matter how difficult the journey is, I will not give up on my dream job.

179. I am freeing myself from my past rejections. I accept the fact that not everyone can appreciate my true worth.
180. I have the power to change the course of my career.
181. I am confident that I can achieve anything once I set my mind to it.
182. I am trained to execute plans properly.
183. I can do anything, but I cannot do everything. I trust my colleagues enough so I can delegate the tasks well.
184. A failure is not the end of my career. I can bounce back and use it to my advantage.
185. I am learning to convey my ideas and feelings better to my boss and my team.
186. Every day I wake up full of aspirations and dreams.
187. Asking for help is not a weakness.
188. I do all the tasks handed to me with max concentration, energy, and effort.
189. The more I grow in my career, the happier I become.
190. I perform better every time I take time to recharge my passion and motivation for work. Self-care is a must.
191. I am driven by my personal motivation to succeed and not by the need to prove myself.
192. My work not only transforms me but also the world.
193. I am born with the mind of a great entrepreneur.

194. I have a powerful business mindset that is the real asset of the company.
195. I am always prepared to face the unpredictable.
196. I attract abundance, prosperity, and wealth into my life.
197. The world needs to see me shine. I am done hiding behind my shell. I am ready to show them what I got.
198. I am a true goal-getter. I see to it that I achieve my ambitions in life.
199. I am the architect of my career. I plan, and I make it a reality.
200. I need no shortcuts. I can achieve my life ambitions by my own set of rules.

150 POSITIVE AFFIRMATIONS FOR HAPPINESS

TIP FROM THE AUTHOR:
Your happiness is something you do for yourself. Own it because it's your birthright.

1. I wake up every morning feeling grateful for my existence, including the color and race I was born with.
2. I unceasingly thank the universe for the life I am living.
3. I deserve to be happy and to feel loved.
4. I feel the excitement surging inside me, thinking of ways to spend a new day.
5. I am committed to doing things that make me feel good.
6. I am filling my mind with positive thoughts of myself.
7. Today, I promise to appreciate myself more.
8. I will always choose myself and my happiness.
9. I am putting all the negative thoughts, memories, and opinions behind me.
10. I fall in love every day with my existence.
11. I am a black man who is sensitive to his own feelings and the feelings of others. I refuse to become a traditional macho man.
12. I am going to live this day to the fullest.
13. I welcome each day with a grateful heart and a positive mind.
14. I am enough. I am loved. I deserve all the happiness in the world.

15. I am a man of color. I am born with a meaningful life. I am determined to make the most of this life every day.
16. I radiate positivity. I am choosing happiness, success, and wealth every day.
17. Every human being has the right to be happy and free.
18. I am ready to welcome joy into my life.
19. I am preparing my mind, body, and heart to attract higher levels of happiness.
20. The most important thing to me right now is my feelings. I will chase after things that make me feel good about myself.
21. All my feelings are valid. I process them one step at a time.
22. As I unravel my feelings, I am learning to love myself all throughout.
23. This is the time to concentrate on my happiness.
24. I am opening myself to becoming happier each day.
25. I am inviting a deeper sense of fulfillment, gratitude, and joy into my life.
26. I am letting go of my hurtful past. I will not let it affect my present and future.
27. The world is big. I can source my happiness in many places available.
28. I will seize every day and make it my own.
29. I accept that sadness is part of life. Happiness would not be able to exist without it.

30. There is no good or bad emotion. All my emotions bear value. They matter to the totality of my existence.
31. I am not wasting my energy worrying about what might go wrong. I am choosing faith over fear.
32. I am channeling all my energy into manifesting my happiness.
33. It is okay to let go. It is okay to let life happen to me.
34. Happiness is coming into my life! I am ready for it.
35. I take responsibility for choosing what thoughts linger in my mind. And I am choosing thoughts that will support my well-being and my joy.
36. I am embracing the thoughts that empower and strengthen me.
37. I am the master of my feelings. I have the power to choose happiness every day, even just for a short time.
38. I confront all my emotions. I acknowledge that to heal emotionally, I must learn to embrace both positive and negative emotions in me.
39. I will continue to nurture optimism in my everyday life.
40. I will dedicate time to taking care of myself physically, mentally, and emotionally.
41. I am allowing myself to play, laugh, and have fun.
42. I deserve to feel joy and positivity unapologetically.

43. I acknowledge the need to set new perspectives so I can achieve happiness.
44. I am enjoying the journey of discovering myself and my happiness.
45. Every day, it gets easier and easier to achieve positivity, fulfillment, and gratitude.
46. I shift away from my focus on the things that hurt me. I decide to actively look for the things I love.
47. I realize now that I should be grateful for many aspects of my life. Now, I am focusing my energy on embracing and appreciating them.
48. I am releasing myself from false judgments, internal pressure, and unnecessary burden.
49. I will continue nurturing genuine connections with my family and friends. I recognize that they are also contributors to my happiness and well-being.
50. I am determined to create a wonderful life for myself.
51. I owe it to myself to become happy and content. It is on me to make my positive imagination my reality.
52. Happiness will naturally flow into my life. I am welcoming it with open arms.
53. I will see to it that happiness becomes part of my daily goals.
54. Happiness is a vital component of my self-care routine. I promise to stick with it religiously.

"Self-care is giving the world the best of you, instead of what is left of you."
— Katie Reed.

55. I am encouraging myself to think of happy thoughts.
56. I thrive on memories that make me feel loved and appreciated.
57. Self-empowerment begins in our minds. I will create and cultivate stories that project a happy me.
58. It is my responsibility to look for the things that make me happy. No one else can do it besides me.
59. I work hard to get to know myself, including my likes and my dislikes.
60. When I am joyful, other positive things will soon come my way.
61. As I become more positive each day, people around me also become happier.
62. I am celebrating my existence in the world. I am celebrating my achievements, no matter how small or big they are. I am deserving of praise and recognition.
63. I am more than ready to ride the happiness in my life.
64. My eyes are always open to new thoughts, especially when I feel stuck and powerless.
65. I will enjoy all the beauty, joy, and excitement that the world has to offer.
66. It is completely okay to prioritize myself and my happiness. I will continue to live this way without feeling sorry.

67. Life is beautiful. I just have to open all my senses to realize this.
68. I will spend more of my time doing the things that make me feel good.
69. I am allowed to feel happy unconditionally.
70. I will continuously nurture my state of joy. I will prevent anything or anyone who attempts to disrupt it.
71. The moment I allow myself to become happy, I am also inspiring others to feel the same.
72. The best time to start the journey of happiness is NOW.
73. My existence shines even brighter when I am happy.
74. It is okay not to be okay.
75. I am not worried about the future. I can maintain this pace and continue being happy about my life.
76. I stay in the moment and savor the happiness it brings me.
77. There is always peace in life. All I have to do is to organize my life and realize it.
78. Positivity comes through when I think simply of life.
79. I am ready to listen to my heart. It perfectly knows where my greatest joys are.
80. I am choosing to rise above negativity.
81. I let my values, principles, and dreams guide my life. I believe that everything will follow.
82. It is completely okay to want more happiness.

83. Happiness will never be lost. It will find me even during the darkest of times.
84. Life is too short to worry about, so I am choosing to trust the process.
85. I will be kind to myself - to my mind, to my heart, and to my body. I will stop being the harshest critique of myself.
86. I appreciate with a grateful heart all the good opportunities, chances, and blessings coming my way.
87. I am thankful to all the people who support my joy and positivity.
88. I am sticking to a set of habits that cultivate a happy mind.
89. I am committed to protecting my happiness and my peace.
90. I am dedicating a special place within me for the safekeeping of my happiness and joy.
91. I will always try to live in the present, letting go fully of my anxiety, worries, and fear.
92. Every moment, every day, every week, every year is a brand new chance to become happy.
93. I will always choose to be my best version, no matter how hard the situation may be.
94. I can always return to my empowered state. Distractions and challenges naturally come and go. It is always up to me to find my peace and my joy.
95. My happiness clears my mind of unnecessary thoughts, which leads me to better decisions.

96. No matter what season I'm in, I always succeed in finding my joys.
97. The only direction I go is forward. I always choose to move on from the things that scared me.
98. I believe with all my heart that the best is yet to come.
99. Being a black man is not easy, but I know good things are a few breaths away from me.
100. Today is the perfect day to show the world how radiant and bright I can be.
101. I will never back away from my happiness.
102. I am recording with my mind all the good things that happened in my life. They are proof of how this life has blessed me.
103. I will always be appreciative of the good things coming my way. I believe that gratitude is the key to true happiness.
104. In times of doubt and chaos, I pursue the decision that gives me peace of mind.
105. I am the conductor of my life. I have full control over the tone of my life. I make sure that my life maintains a lively tone.
106. No matter how hard today was, tomorrow will be another chance at happiness.
107. My life is a testament to joy, fulfillment, and peace.
108. Today, I am serving others with the joy I am feeling.
109. Happiness is better felt when shared with others.

110. I appreciate my body, my skin, and my abilities the way it is. There is no better version than how I look today.
111. Judgment has no place in my life. I refuse to be manipulated by what other people want me to look like.
112. I am extremely grateful for all the emotions I am feeling. It allows me to experience great things in life.
113. I cannot control everything around me, but I can always control how I will feel about them.
114. I am breaking free from the internal restraints I placed on myself. The only way to become truly happy is to be free.
115. Every day, I am learning more and more about my happiness.
116. Although life is not candy, I always choose to be optimistic.
117. I am allowing all my love to flow inside and guide me towards my joy.
118. There is no limit to how much happiness I can get. The more, the better.
119. I always deserve more and never less.
120. I can access the part of me that has always remained still and at ease. It is the key to true inner peace.
121. Happiness is my friend, and I am welcoming it to my life with grace.
122. My joy stems from kindness.

123. Comparison will never do any good to my happiness.
124. I will prevent my self-judgment from stopping me achieve an empowered state.
125. I am proud of how my life is currently going. It has never been better!
126. My life just keeps on going in the right direction.
127. Doing fun things will eventually lead me to happiness.
128. I am always listening to myself. I am the only person who can unravel my true happiness.
129. I am stronger than the things that make me sad and lonely.
130. I am braver than my fears and worries.
131. My peace is stronger than the negativity my mind is trying to imagine.
132. I can be happy often.
133. I can live my life with a peaceful heart.
134. I can attract positivity and optimism.
135. I can succeed in my journey.
136. I can love myself better.
137. I can bring happiness and kindness to others.
138. I can transform my life no matter how hard the hurdles I face.
139. I am forgiving myself because I want to be free and happy.
140. The best gift I can give to myself is inner peace.
141. Anything becomes possible when I am happy and faithful.

142. I am surrounded by reliable people who are always ready to help.
143. I am accepted and loved by many. I will never be lonely on this journey.
144. A state of joy is a type of lifestyle I choose to practice.
145. I will smile more. I will laugh often. I will think positively always.
146. Taking care of myself is manly. I am strong, and I acknowledge the need to rest and meditate.
147. Happiness is a seed inside that I will continue nurturing.
148. It's time to dump my emotional baggage. I am only keeping the things that support my well-being.
149. The first step in achieving happiness is the willingness to feel it.
150. Being happy is a continuous effort. I must keep my will and effort alive.

150 AFFIRMATIONS FOR LOVE AND RELATIONSHIPS

"One day, someone will walk into your life and make you see why it never worked out with anyone else."

1. I can find love because I love and fully accept myself.
2. I am born a black man, and I am proud of it. I believe that any human being like me deserves love and acceptance from another.
3. I am black, and I am more than worthy of love.
4. I attract good, caring, and understanding people in my life.
5. I am mentally and emotionally ready to open my heart to another person.
6. I can find the right person for me - someone who sees and treat me as an equal.
7. I believe that I can meet my soulmate at the right time.
8. I can find love because I am ready to share mine.
9. I am loved in the way I have always wanted.
10. I am dedicating a space in my life for my special one.
11. The universe will conspire in my favor. It will bring me to my soulmate soon.
12. I am permitting myself to receive and give love.
13. I am very lovable. Any person would be lucky to have a partner.
14. My heart is strong, kind, and forgiving. It is more than ready to love and be loved.
15. My doors are open to people who are willing to be part of my life.
16. I deserve passionate and intense love like everybody else.
17. I deserve to be treated with the utmost respect in a relationship.

18. I deserve a faithful partner who values loyalty as much as I do.
19. I deserve a kind of relationship that supports me and my aspirations in life. I will never settle for anything less.
20. I always love, honestly.
21. I attract a long-term relationship that works for a promising future.
22. My life is overflowing with true love.
23. I feel complete and thankful for my partner. His/her company has truly been life-changing.
24. We are working together to build a strong and loving relationship.
25. I am ready to compromise and sacrifice in the name of love.
26. I value the feelings and well-being of my partner.
27. I feel truly blessed with the gift of genuine love.
28. I feel more confident about myself when I am surrounded by people who love me.
29. I value the time and moments I share with my soulmate.
30. Every second with my partner is precious.
31. Everything is equal in our relationship. I totally respect his/her boundaries as he/she does mine.
32. I am letting go of my past heartbreaks. They will never hurt me again.
33. I will never settle for anyone who does not respect and value me appropriately.

34. I will continue to nurture the relationship we built. I will remain a loving, caring, and understanding partner.
35. I am committed to staying with my partner for a very long time.
36. I refuse to be influenced by others' opinions of my partner. The only opinion that matters is mine.
37. My partner helps me become a better version of myself every day.
38. Whatever comes our way, I believe that we can overcome it. We are strong.
39. I strive to make my partner safe in my company.
40. I am learning to love myself, so I can love others fully.
41. I know that somewhere in the universe, my soulmate is waiting for me too.
42. I can attract a kind, strong, and loving person who will see me the way I want to be seen.
43. I am in a relationship where I do not have to compete for her attention and time.
44. I refuse to settle with a person that makes me feel unsafe and insecure.
45. I am not afraid of love. I am not afraid of a relationship. I am not afraid to make myself available.
46. I am a person who inspires my partner to become the best version of herself.
47. I practice healthy and open communication with the people I love.

48. I feel fulfilled and at peace in my current relationship.
49. I am a man who is strong enough to express his emotions and affection.
50. I always try to make my partner happy.
51. I am in a relationship that values the importance of trust.
52. I am careful in making decisions regarding my love life.
53. I refuse to rush into things I am not ready for. I will not be dragged by peer pressure. I let my relationship progress step by step.
54. I will experience a love that blows my mind and touches my soul.
55. I will not settle for fake and fleeting love.
56. I will keep my promises to my partner.
57. I will take care of my partner so she does not feel lonely.
58. I will continue to nurture my hope that someday, the right person will come along.
59. I refuse to become someone I am, not for the person I love.
60. I am going to be the best person for my partner.
61. I will be a pillar of strength to my special one.
62. I can show both my strengths and flaws to my partner without feeling scared.
63. I will be supportive of my partner's dreams in life.
64. I allow my partner to show her true self to me. I will not judge her.

65. I will be the one to initiate conversations that matter. I will talk with my partner respectfully, especially when things are difficult.
66. I am a man of color who can love another person in the best way possible.
67. I am in a relationship that helps me heal my past wounds.
68. I will be the kind of partner I have always dreamed of.
69. I am in a relationship that makes me feel good about myself.
70. I am a logical man. I will not act based on my emotions alone.
71. I am a man who is sure of himself.
72. I prepared myself well before committing to a relationship. I made sure to heal myself by filling my voids with hope, love, and faith.
73. I have already put my past behind me. They would not hurt my partner and me. I will always try to stay in the moment.
74. My present life is filled with people who I love so dearly.
75. I will attract a partner who will accept the worst and best parts of me.
76. I will definitely be happy in my next relationship.
77. I am a good man. I am sure that a better person will love me.
78. I am forgiving myself for all the mistakes I have made in my previous relationships.

79. I will always try to prevent myself from repeating the same mistakes. I will be a better man.
80. I will give my partner her space. I am a man who values her freedom to express herself individually.
81. I will always hold my partner's hand in every life battle.
82. I am in a relationship that discusses things openly and maturely.
83. I am a man who thinks of his partner's feelings seriously.
84. My heart is happy with the person I am with.
85. I always think of a future for my partner and me.
86. I never give up on love so easily.
87. I am confident that my heart is fully recovered from all that it has been through.
88. I never stop being a good person to my partner.
89. Human connections will come naturally to me.
90. I am grateful for the person I am with today.
91. I will keep on making my partner feel how thankful I am for her existence.
92. I love every aspect of my partner. The more I get to know her, the more I fall in love.
93. I trust that the universe will bring me to the person who will love and appreciate me every day of my life.
94. I deserve a person who is ready to listen to my stories and feelings.

95. I am choosing to surround myself with people who truly love me. I will not be bothered by people who try to drag me down.
96. No matter how my life can be challenging, love is always possible.
97. Every moment I spend with my partner is a treasured memory.
98. Even though I love myself, I know when to be selfless for my partner. I believe that this is the essence of true love.
99. My love respects my partner's boundaries. It will never suffocate nor compel my partner to do something she does not agree with.
100. I make sure to ask for her consent in everything we do together.
101. I express my love through kindness, thoughtfulness, and forgiveness.
102. My ears are always open for her silent pleas, side of the stories, and worries.
103. I acknowledge that love is not easy, but anything can succeed when we work together.
104. I am worthy of a person who respects my boundaries and limitations.
105. I am a good man, and I deserve self-less and encompassing love.
106. I deserve a relationship where I can be vulnerable.
107. I deserve a person who will comfort me during difficult times.

108. I am a good man who consoles his partner in times of vulnerability.
109. I practice forgiveness in my relationship. I believe that everyone deserves a second chance.
110. I am worthy of a relationship that allows me to commit mistakes without judgment.
111. I deserve a partner who goes out of her way to make me feel loved.
112. A true, selfless, and encompassing love starts within me.
113. I am a good man that radiates love.
114. I always try to spread love everywhere I go.
115. I do little and grand things to make my partner feel loved.
116. I feel love. I understand love. I express love.
117. Our relationship is strong. We can overcome whatever comes our way.
118. With every hurdle we overcome, our relationship becomes stronger.
119. Our love grows stronger and deeper each passing day.
120. I never give up on a relationship without trying everything I could.
121. I deserve a partner who will love me through the hard times.
122. Every day is a new chance for me to meet my soulmate.
123. Every day is a new day to become a better partner.
124. I am a good friend to my partner.

125. I deserve to be in a relationship that treasures my existence and my love.
126. I will be strong enough to let off a person who I know is not good for me.
127. I will always be brave to walk away from abusive and bad relationships.
128. I only deserve the best in the world.
129. I will love in a smart way. I refuse to throw everything for the sake of so-called "love."
130. Even though I am a man, I am allowed to be slow and careful in choosing my partner.
131. I deserve a relationship where everything is given and received equally,
132. I am overflowing with love that I am willing to share with another person.
133. I deserve a partner who will inspire and support me in the goals I am building.
134. I deserve a partner who values and nurtures my peace.
135. I refuse to be mistreated in any way.
136. I respect my partner as much as I respect myself.
137. I will always be kind to my partner. I will never resort to violence and hurtful words.
138. I deserve a partner who recognizes my strengths and praises me for them.
139. I am letting go of all my bitterness, anger, and regrets from my past relationships.

140. I am a good man who can control his anger well. I refuse to be manipulated by such negative emotions.
141. I know very well that love is not codependency. Love is freeing.
142. I am a responsible man. I will never make excuses for my shortcomings and mistakes.
143. Strength is measured through accountability. I will be brave enough to say "sorry" when at fault.
144. My pride as a man does not rule me or my relationship.
145. I will not let my insecurities and issues sabotage my relationship.
146. I am a loyal man.
147. Our love always wins, no matter how hard the circumstance is.
148. Love for myself does not diminish when I share it with another person. It grows.
149. I am a man who is brave enough to be passionate and intimate with another person.
150. I refuse to be controlled by desperation for love. I accept that everything happens in due time.

100 Affirmations for Health and Wellness

TIP FROM THE AUTHOR:

Health is wealth that never gets old. The only way you make the most out of your life is if you are healthy enough to live through it.

1. I am a proud man of color that values his health and physique very much.
2. I am a man worthy of a healthy and well-functioning body.
3. I am a healthy and energetic man.
4. I am working hard to build and nurture a healthy body.
5. I am a man who knows his body well.
6. I understand what my body needs, and I exert effort to meet them.
7. I always put my health and well-being as my top priority.
8. I am a strong-willed man who takes in-charge of his own health.
9. I am the only person who can decide on what type of body I should have.
10. I have a strong, beautiful, and healthy body.
11. I love my body, and I will work on preserving it well.
12. I acknowledge that my body and health need improvement.
13. I am thankful for my body and my energy. It allows me to live my life fully.
14. I connect with every cell of my body through a healthy diet and regular exercise.
15. I fall in love with my body every day.
16. I acknowledge the uniqueness of my own body.
17. I always pay attention to what my body needs.

18. I dedicate time and resources to making my body strong and healthy.
19. I intend to have a healthy body for the rest of my life.
20. I always wake up full of energy and optimism.
21. I am fit. I am strong. I am power.
22. Exercising regularly makes me healthier and stronger every day.
23. Every exercise rep I do is a step closer to my ideal body shape.
24. I will not be distracted. I will keep working out for my body.
25. I will do extra laps, reps, and cycles today.
26. I feel better every time I move my body.
27. I will attain all my fitness goals.
28. I work hard to stay in shape for myself and the people who love me.
29. I become a better version of myself every time I eat healthily.
30. I make sure that my body can fight off diseases around me.
31. I treat my body the way it deserves, with utmost care.
32. I feel the power flowing naturally inside me. I can achieve all my body goals.
33. I fill my body with energy through regular exercise and a balanced diet.
34. I drink fluids all the time to keep my body clean and my mind clear.

35. I refuse to let unhealthy foods from entering my system.
36. Anything that is done too much will do nothing but bad to my body.
37. I pay attention to the changes occurring in my body.
38. I surround myself with people who support my health and wellness.
39. I crave highly nutritious food.
40. I will stop eating too many sweets, alcohol, and salty foods.
41. I love eating vegetables and fruits. I will not get tired of having them.
42. I always study how to make my body healthier and more energetic.
43. I enjoy working hard to strengthen my muscles and bones.
44. I never get tired from exercising.
45. I love being physically active. It boosts my energy.
46. I make sure to sleep on time. I believe that sleep is essential for my well-being.
47. I always sleep for 8 hours a day.
48. I meditate regularly to release stress.
49. My mental health is as important as my physical health.
50. I train myself to think healthily.
51. I make my mind stronger so it can lead my body to a healthier future.

52. I am grateful for the great connection between my mind and my body.
53. I live in a nice environment that supports my health and wealth.
54. The nutrients I eat flow naturally in my body.
55. Investing in my health is the best thing I will do today.
56. Today is a new day to gain energy, power, and wellness.
57. I show my love for my body by eating nutritious food and exercising regularly.
58. I always make healthy choices for myself.
59. I attract good and healthy energy.
60. I refrain from making habits that harm my body.
61. I inhale healthy energy. I exhale stress and toxins.
62. Good health is my birthright and my responsibility.
63. I prioritize my rest. I believe that rest is progress.
64. I am well-rested and energized. I can do everything I set my mind to.
65. Healthy living is a choice I make every day.
66. I can move freely because of all the physical activities I am doing.
67. Good health is a gift I give to myself every day.
68. I am committed to eating foods full of vitamins, minerals, and proteins.
69. I respect my body fully, so I am doing my best to keep it healthy.

70. I focus my attention on the things that are good for my body.
71. I feel happy and fulfilled every time I exercise.
72. I exercise to feel good about myself, not the other way around.
73. I feel rewarded for every good change happening to my body.
74. Water is my sustenance. I drink more than 8 glasses of water every day.
75. I stick to a regular sleeping cycle to allow my cells to recuperate.
76. I always crave new healthy experiences.
77. I strive to keep my healthy relationship with my body for a long time.
78. I can recover quickly from any injury and sickness.
79. The only direction I go is towards wellness and fitness.
80. I am attractive because I am healthy.
81. I enjoy living my life because I am healthy and free of diseases.
82. I attract good energy because of my healthy body.
83. My immune system is strong. It can fight off any threat that comes my way.
84. The healthier I get, the happier and more attractive I become.
85. A sexy body is a healthy body.

86. I get closer to my dream body every time I exercise and eat right.
87. Today, I will lose unhealthy fats.
88. My lungs are stronger than ever. Thanks to all the cardio I am doing.
89. Today, I have decided to go extend my limits. Instead of 5 laps, I will run 10.
90. Exercising gives me comfort and satisfaction. I have never felt this good.
91. MY hard work will pay off soon. I will see the scales tipping in my favor.
92. My fitness journey can be steady and slow. I acknowledge that losing weight and building muscles take time.
93. I feel the momentum building up in my body.
94. Working out relieves my stress and fatigue.
95. I always make time for my regular exercise, no matter how busy I am.
96. I have the discipline to stick to my exercise routine and balanced diet.
97. I get stronger for every rep I execute.
98. I challenge myself and what I can do every time I exercise.
99. I have the stamina to run more laps today.
100. I always feel motivated and driven to exercise.

100 AFFIRMATIONS FOR INVESTMENTS, BUSINESS, AND FINANCIAL SUCCESS

"Don't worry about being successful but work toward being significant, and the success will naturally follow."
-*Oprah Winfrey*

1. I am born a money magnet. Financial success is my birthright.
2. I welcome financial stability, prosperity, and abundance into my life.
3. Money is flowing naturally into my life.
4. I am letting go of the things that stop money from coming through my life.
5. I am a man of color that is born with good fortune in business.
6. I am working hard to achieve financial stability and freedom.
7. I am closer to financial stability today than I was yesterday.
8. I am learning to limit my expenses.
9. My top priority is to save as much money as possible.
10. I know the value of money very well, and I make sure to spend it wisely.
11. I am constantly looking for new ways to grow my money.
12. I am wealthy in so many ways.
13. Wealth and prosperity are coming to me.
14. Every day is a new day to find new opportunities for me to grow my wealth.
15. I am a man of color, and I deserve to live a well-provided and wealthy life.
16. I recognize the vital role of money in a comfortable life.

17. My finances do not intimidate me because I have a concrete management plan.
18. I am a very capable man who can overcome any financial obstacles that come my way.
19. I get closer and closer to my financial goals every day.
20. I have the mind, the power, and the discipline to become financially successful someday.
21. I am building a solid financial foundation for my future wealth.
22. I have a positive relationship with my money.
23. The cash flows positively into my life.
24. Generosity is an important ingredient to financial success.
25. I have the mind to make my money bigger than it was today.
26. I pour a reasonable amount of my time, effort, and resources to grow my money.
27. I trust myself and my abilities in looking for worthy investments.
28. Limitless investments are waiting for me. I just have to open my doors.
29. I believe that I can achieve all my financial goals, and I will.
30. All my hard work and investments will pay off in time. Patience is key.
31. I always choose to be practical in my purchases.
32. I make it a habit to budget my money smartly.

33. There are a million ways to enjoy life while on a budget.
34. I will be brave enough to make tough financial decisions today because I know I can reap its fruit in the future.
35. I am starting an emergency fund today. I acknowledge its importance to my safety.
36. I am the only person who has control over my finances and investments.
37. I have control over my expenditures. I will only spend it on things that truly matter.
38. Every dollar I save and cultivate is a step closer to financial success.
39. I am a well-informed and responsible spender.
40. I am committed to paying off all my debts.
41. I intend to build my wealth at a young age so I can enjoy it earlier.
42. I am taking the first step to prosperity by studying the basics of finances and investments. I believe that knowledge is power.
43. I am always excited about embracing new opportunities to grow my money.
44. I am bigger than my financial struggles. I will not be defeated by it. I will succeed.
45. I believe that my current financial situation will get better.
46. I set financial goals, and I work hard to attain them.
47. I will turn my financial dreams into reality.

48. I track my expenses religiously. I acknowledge that this is an important practice for financial success.
49. I have a strong will. I will not be tempted by unnecessary expenditures.
50. Great opportunities are continuously flowing into my business.
51. This will be a productive day. My business will generate more money today.
52. I am manifesting the success of my business.
53. I always establish a comprehensive business plan so that my company is well guided.
54. I am the best person who can run my company.
55. I have a sharp sense of good investments. My intuition has never failed me.
56. I become a better business for every struggle I overcome.
57. I always make business decisions that generate more income.
58. Every dollar that I invest in my business will turn into millions someday.
59. Today is a new day to earn bigger revenues.
60. I refuse to throw out money on unimportant things. Investments take the highest precedence.
61. I am keeping my capital in check so that my business runs smoothly.
62. My mind can create profit-earning ideas.
63. I am manifesting the expansion of my business this year. Anything is possible with hard work and determination.

64. My business is destined for a brighter future.
65. My guts always lead my business to worthy investments.
66. My business can succeed in every way possible.
67. I use my time wisely. I only use it in money-generating projects.
68. The universe has a lot of opportunities in store for my business.
69. My business will become big soon.
70. I make decisions on investments using a clear and rational mind.
71. I am in full control of my finances and investments. I assess my options as well as risks carefully.
72. I am knowledgeable of my finances and the market.
73. I let smart choices fill my mind.
74. I listen with an open mind to my trusted financial advisers.
75. I am a capable investor. My stocks always rise in value.
76. Investments come naturally to me. It's like I was born to do it.
77. I have eyes for long-term investments that will prosper in the future.
78. I prioritize activities that generate profits.
79. All the money that I invest will grow exponentially.
80. I only manage my finances. I refuse to be controlled by money.

81. I am always up for the challenge of earning more money.
82. Making money does not feel like work. I enjoy every moment of it.
83. I am working hard to live by the essence of financial literacy.
84. I am committed to only taking worthy risks when it comes to investments.
85. I keep tabs on the current trends in the market.
86. I feel extremely optimistic about all my investments.
87. My brain is wired to take calculated risks.
88. I am continuously researching investments.
89. I am a smart, well-informed, and skilled investor.
90. I am working hard to nurture an investor mindset.
91. I will continue to persevere so I can achieve my investment goals.
92. I recognize that the only way to grow money is through investments.
93. I am working hard on preparing my mind and heart for business.
94. I take great pride in my investment decisions.
95. I am getting better and better at investing as time goes by.
96. My investments have the potential to grow big in the future.
97. I am patient with my investments. Being financially successful does not happen overnight.
98. I love investing my money in several industries.

99. I will continue working hard until I master the art of investments and stocks.
100. I focus my energy and mind on achieving financial success.

50 AFFIRMATIONS FOR CREATIVITY

Creativity doesn't wait for that perfect moment. It fashions its own perfect moments out of ordinary ones.
— *Bruce Garrabrandt*

1. I am a talented black man who is full of creative ideas.
2. There is innate creativity and ingenuity in every project I do.
3. Creativity flows naturally in every cell of my body.
4. I am born to create innovative solutions to today's problems.
5. I am born to create amazing things.
6. My creativity and intelligence power every decision I make.
7. It is my birthright to follow my creative pursuits.
8. My mind easily connects me with all the inspirations available to the world.
9. I let my imagination take me to greater heights.
10. Novel and creative ideas come naturally to me wherever I go.
11. No one has the same mind as mine. My thought process is unique; so are my ideas.
12. I am grateful for my imagination, which allows me to think of innovative solutions.
13. I can find inspiration in any environment I am in.
14. I am attracting good and creative ideas today.
15. I am always excited to think and create.
16. I am focusing my mind and my energy on making innovative activities.
17. The universe gives me a plentiful supply of inspiration. I just have to embrace them openly.
18. I am learning every day how to cultivate and nurture my creativity.

19. I will make bright new ideas today.
20. I enjoy the challenge of making and creating.
21. I am becoming more creative and innovative as the day goes by.
22. My creative potential is limitless. I can create whatever I set my mind to.
23. I welcome all the ideas coming my way.
24. I am an innovator. I am a thinker.
25. I never settle for mediocre ideas. I always go to extra lengths to think of top-notch solutions.
26. I am a man of color gifted with brilliant ideas.
27. I can always make innovative solutions to every problem I encounter.
28. I can overcome every dead end I face in my creative journey.
29. I never ran out of big and creative ideas.
30. My creativity knows no limits.
31. Fresh ideas will always come to me naturally.
32. I fully believe in my mind and my abilities.
33. I trust my creative sense and where it leads me.
34. I always enjoy thinking outside the box. It is my forte.
35. I radiate so much creativity that it inspires people around me.
36. I am freeing myself from all the distractions that block my creativity.
37. My creative ideas are deserving of recognition.
38. I feel overflowing enthusiasm for creating effective solutions and innovative ideas.

39. I am exercising my creativity every minute of every day.
40. My creativity can soar to the greater heights of life.
41. I find it very easy to make my ideas into reality.
42. I am a man who feels very passionate about his creative works.
43. I enjoy every step of my creative process.
44. I am an intelligent man, and I can do well in everything I do.
45. I am growing to become a better artist as the day goes by.
46. My amazing works will soon be appreciated by the world.
47. My eyes let me see the true beauty of the world.
48. I unceasingly express my creativity.
49. I am stronger than my criticisms. I always believe that my skills and ideas can get better.
50. I am an amazing artist and innovator waiting to be discovered.

50 Affirmations for Academic Success

Point to Ponder:
There is no one in this world who can do so much for you than you. So, grab the world and show the people what you can do. The pinnacle of success is waiting for you.

1. I am born with an intelligent mind.
2. I have a unique mind. No one can replicate the way I think and learn new concepts.
3. I can ace any test if I study smart.
4. I enjoy the time I spend in school. Learning is an adventure I never get tired of.
5. I have a strong and sharp memory that can retain information.
6. I am manifesting good grades this semester.
7. I am a black man who works hard for his dreams.
8. I have good study habits. It always gives me outstanding results.
9. I am a good student because I am responsible.
10. Studying comes naturally to me. I always do well with it.
11. I have full control over my grades. I will not let my grades control me or my life.
12. I am a bright student full of enthusiasm for learning.
13. I become a better student day by day.
14. Today, I woke up with a new motivation to go to school and learn about new things.
15. I refuse to be dragged down by my failures. I will move past them and study better.
16. I am directing all my focus and energy into my studies. I will pass the exam.
17. I can do well on this test because I am prepared. Preparation is the key.

18. I refused to be distracted. I take my schedules and study plans very seriously.
19. I acknowledge the truth that studies are the gateway to my dreams.
20. I am setting aside my fears and insecurities. I know I can do well.
21. I am a highly capable man who can achieve all my educational goals.
22. I continuously cultivate my knowledge because learning never stops.
23. I am studying well. I am studying regularly. And I will continue to do so until I reach my dreams.
24. I can understand all the concepts today, no matter how hard and confusing they may be.
25. I feel relaxed whenever I am taking an exam. I do not allow pressure to take me over.
26. I always prioritize my education.
27. I organize my studying habits regularly. I make sure that they remain effective and up-to-date.
28. I will not let anything or anyone stop me from excelling in school. I am destined for the best.
29. Studying comes with its challenges, but I believe in myself. I know that I can overcome them.
30. Today is a new day to get better at studying.
31. I love all my subjects, so I am dedicating equal amounts of effort to each.
32. I enjoy participating in study groups because they help me collect my thoughts.

33. Being a man of color will not stop me from being the best student that I can possibly be.
34. I am studying because of my sheer passion for learning.
35. I am embracing all the new concepts coming to me.
36. My mind absorbs all the new information easily.
37. I am a model student, and I will continue to be.
38. I am dedicating five hours of my day to studying.
39. I always celebrate my academic successes, no matter how small they are.
40. I am forgiving myself for the mistakes I made in the past. Every day is a new day to improve my grades.
41. I am a student. I do not fear asking for help from my professors and classmates. Learning is best enjoyed when shared.
42. I always offer my help to my classmates.
43. My self-confidence grows with my expanding knowledge.
44. My brain cells are functioning well. They are actively transmitting the information.
45. I will not be overcome by stress, pressure, and anxiety. I will remain calm in the face of exams and recitations.
46. There is no greater joy for me than discovering and learning about new things.
47. I will succeed in my studies.
48. I am choosing to prioritize my studies today.

49. I always set high standards for my education.
50. My greatest pride is my beautiful and capable mind.

50 Affirmations for Spiritual Awakening, Alignment, and Growth

1. I am a black man born on this beautiful planet. And I possess an innate connection with the world.
2. I have a spirit that is fully enlightened and blessed.
3. I am a man who emanates serenity, love, and spirituality.
4. The universe's abundance flows naturally within me.
5. I am with the universe. I am with nature.
6. I allow the Divine to intervene in my life.
7. My spirit radiates brightly and warms the people around me.
8. I am offering myself to the universe. I permit it to act on its behalf.
9. I believe that my inner peace will nurture my wisdom.
10. I am born with a purpose. No one can do it besides me, so I will live life honestly and responsibly.
11. My spirit is the source of my love, wisdom, and truth.
12. Nothing will ever break my spirit.
13. My eyes always seek beauty in other people and in this world.
14. I trust in my inner guidance and moral compass. They never lead me astray.
15. I am cultivating a deeper sense of inner peace.
16. I have a beautiful soul that attracts good people.
17. My energy is in complete sync with the universe.

18. Every day I nurture my connection to the world through regular meditation.
19. My life is a blessing to the world.
20. I believe that everything that is happening in my life has a purpose.
21. I breathe in life, peace, and joy in my body.
22. I feel completely connected to my soul.
23. I am a spiritual person who appreciates the real beauty of this world.
24. I openly embrace the guidance from the divine.
25. I am one of His creations. I am loved. I am cherished.
26. My high spiritual consciousness guides me to better decisions in life.
27. I am opening my doors and windows for all the Divine's blessings.
28. I am in perfect sync with the world and its energy.
29. I am power because love flows through me.
30. I am enveloped by the grace of a higher being.
31. I have full trust in what the universe has in store for me.
32. I am a blessed man.
33. I am ready to connect with my innermost self.
34. My life is proof of the kindness of the universe.
35. I am grateful for all the good things happening in my life.
36. The universe is helping me reach my aspirations in life.
37. I am working hard for my spiritual growth.

38. The only person in control of my spirituality is me.
39. Today, I will listen more to my intuition.
40. My body is home to a peaceful and loving soul.
41. I trust that the Divine will help me in every hardship I face.
42. I was born beautiful, and I will live showing my beauty to the world.
43. I am a part of a wonderful world made by the Divine. I deserve to live peacefully and happily.
44. I am entrusting all my worries and fears to the Divine.
45. I am letting love guide my life.
46. I am a spiritual being housed in a human body.
47. I am a man of color blessed with overflowing faith, peace, love, and happiness.
48. All the good things will happen at the Divine's most perfect time.
49. I acknowledge the existence of a higher power.
50. I am inhaling faith and trust. I am exhaling my doubts, fears, and pain.

75 Affirmations for Healing the Soul, Mind, and Body

Healing takes courage, and we all have courage, even if we have to dig a little to find it.
- *Tori Amos*

1. I am stronger than the pain I am feeling right now. I will not be overcome by it.
2. I am the only person who best understands my pain and its cure.
3. I am in full control of my reaction to pain.
4. I welcome all the possible cures to the pain I am feeling.
5. My illness and wound make me a stronger being.
6. I can recover from every injury, illness, or trauma I face.
7. I know that with proper medication and therapy, the pain will go away soon.
8. Pain is a friend that makes me feel more human.
9. Every cell in my body has the power to heal on its own.
10. I am committing myself to all the ways that my body can heal.
11. I take my healing and vitality as my priorities.
12. Today, I am choosing to get and be well.
13. I accept that my body will occasionally be unwell. But I have the power to recover and heal.
14. I am fortunate to have a body capable of recovering from illness and injury.
15. I am letting go of all the things that pain me physically, emotionally, and mentally.
16. I am allowing my soul and mind to heal from the memories and experiences that hurt me in the past.

17. Today, I feel more motivated and determined to heal from my emotional wounds.
18. I am manifesting my emotional, physical, and mental healing.
19. I am manifesting that today will be a better day. I will get past all my traumas.
20. I am a man who deserves healing.
21. My limitations, setbacks, and boundaries do not define me.
22. Today, I decided to stop being a victim. I live like a hero of my own story.
23. I am learning to release my grudge from people who had hurt me in the past.
24. I forgive myself for all the self-sabotaging moments I put myself in.
25. My happiness and peace are a work in progress. I take it one step at a time.
26. Today, I decided to move on from all the heartbreaks I've had.
27. Apart from the valuable lessons, I am leaving my hurtful past behind.
28. My past does not define my present and future.
29. I am learning to live securely and happily with my weaknesses.
30. I have a good feeling that today will be a better day for my emotional, physical, and mental well-being.
31. I am a beautiful mix of my strengths and weaknesses.

32. I accept that my reality will not always be in my favor.
33. I will stop dwelling on my mistakes and try focusing on what I can do to improve as a person.
34. Nothing can cause me emotional pain because I feel safe and secure with myself right now.
35. I fully trust the gradual process of healing. I acknowledge that wounds of any kind do not close up overnight.
36. I have huge respect for myself, so I refuse to drown in my regrets and fears in life.
37. I treat every hurtful experience as an opportunity to grow emotionally, mentally, and spiritually.
38. It is okay to make mistakes. I am a human being, and it's in my nature.
39. I am letting go of my anger because it does not do any good to my life.
40. I am freeing myself from the shackles of my old and sabotaging self.
41. I am closing my mind and heart to hurtful memories and thoughts.
42. Today, I am giving myself a chance to feel better.
43. I refuse to be consumed by my trauma and negative feelings. I am stronger than them.
44. I am healing today. I am feeling better. I am better.
45. I am a miracle. My life is a miracle.
46. Every breath I take is a step towards healing.
47. I am acknowledging all the unresolved feelings I have.

48. I am patient with myself. I understand that healing takes time.
49. Today. I will be kinder to myself.
50. My circumstances are tough, but they will not break me, for I am strong.
51. I am stopping my past from haunting me. It's time that I move on.
52. I am on a wonderful journey of overcoming my hurtful past.
53. I accept that healing is a step-by-step process.
54. Everything I will do today will be for my healing.
55. I am taking one step at a time. Impatience will do me no good.
56. The pain I am feeling today will not last forever. Better days are definitely coming.
57. I am in pursuit of my peace, happiness, and truth.
58. My feelings are valid. It is my birthright to feel and express them.
59. I am not letting anything stop me from emotional healing.
60. I know that this painful experience is teaching me something I can use in the future.
61. I am who I am today because of all the painful experiences in the past.
62. I am directing my energy to my present because it is what truly matters.
63. There is no shame in sharing my feelings. I am surrounded by good people whom I can fully trust.

64. I am grateful for all the challenges that shaped me to become the great person I am today.
65. I am sending forgiveness to people who had hurt me in the past.
66. I will no longer suppress my emotions inside. Expressing them is healthier.
67. My life is just in the beginning, and it does not end with these challenges.
68. I will always choose a path toward my healing.
69. I choose to be kind and patient in these trying times.
70. My life is not complete without challenges.
71. I let my emotions flow and direct me towards my healing.
72. My healing starts the moment I acknowledge and accept my own emotions.
73. What I went through does not define me or my future.
74. Nothing and no one can take away the power that is within me.
75. I am excited to start a fresh new chapter in my life.

200 AFFIRMATIONS FOR STRESS MANAGEMENT, ANXIETY, AND DEPRESSION

Point to Ponder:
Remember that life is meant to be lived, no matter how black and white it seems. Just stick to your best qualities, and everything good will follow.

1. I am a man living in a safe and supportive environment.
2. I am choosing to react positively to everything happening in my life.
3. I am acknowledging the discomfort I am feeling right now.
4. I refuse to linger on the negative thoughts in my head because they will not help me get better.
5. I will not let my anxiety get over me.
6. It is okay that I get anxious. I know that I can overcome it nonetheless.
7. I breathe in peace and relief while I exhale the stress and tension inside me.
8. Today, I am choosing to feel better.
9. I am a capable man of color who can overcome any challenges that may come my way.
10. I have my anxiety under control. I refuse to let it control my life.
11. I am clearing my mind off worries, fears, and other negative thoughts.
12. I am stronger and more dependable than my anxiety.
13. I feel calmer with every breath I take.
14. I am shedding the weight of my worries off my shoulders.
15. I will stop being burdened by my anxiety.
16. Today, I will learn how to relieve my anxiety healthily.

17. I am in control of my life, not the threats around me.
18. My panic attack is subsiding every minute.
19. I am calm and collected. My negative feelings will get better soon.
20. I refuse to let my anxiety decide for me. I am the only master of my destiny.
21. I was born and built to face my fears and worries head-on.
22. My determination and will are stronger than the forces dragging me down.
23. I am surrounded by good people who acknowledge and respect my rights and welfare. So, I will not be afraid.
24. I trust myself. I will always have my back, no matter what.
25. My anxiety is only temporary.
26. I believe that everything will get better soon. I'll just have to continue living my life the best way possible.
27. Today, I prioritize my peace and happiness over my worries and fears.
28. I am safe. I am calm. I am okay.
29. I am not afraid of challenges or changes coming my way. They are natural parts of life.
30. I have nothing to be scared of because I am loved and well-cared for.
31. I will start refusing things that do me no good.

32. Saying no is okay. It does not diminish my essence as a person.
33. I am allowing myself to unwind and rest from the world.
34. I am freeing myself from the toxic and hurtful thoughts plaguing my mind.
35. I have the power to live life peacefully, free from panic and stress.
36. Today, I am choosing to be kind and patient with myself.
37. I am a human who is allowed to commit mistakes. I am not afraid because I can improve.
38. I have survived this panic attack before, and surely, I can do it today.
39. I am a man of color born with a purpose. My existence has a role to play in the universe.
40. Mistakes are room for growth and improvement. I must not be afraid of them.
41. My fears and worries are valid, but they should not linger.
42. I am not alone in this life. I have people who help me in my battles.
43. Loving myself more is not selfishness. It is my birthright.
44. I accept that there are things in life I cannot control, and they should not affect my peace.
45. I am allowed to share my burdens in life.
46. The world is not for me to carry.

47. I acknowledge that I can have good and bad days. That is what life is.
48. Everything will get better because I am born with a good fate.
49. I will feel better one step at a time.
50. There is nothing wrong with prioritizing myself and my welfare.
51. The tension and stress inside me are dissipating.
52. My stress is a temporary thing. It will not last me forever.
53. I am in full control of my stress levels.
54. I can feel my stress level going down.
55. I always choose to respond to stressful situations by being calm and collected.
56. I am a strong man who cannot be overcome by stress.
57. I am trained to handle stressful situations effectively.
58. My decisions will not be influenced by my stress level. I will always be logical and reasonable.
59. Stress relief and relaxation are my birthrights. Nothing and no one can change this fact.
60. Some things will be beyond my control, and I feel okay with this truth.
61. This stressful moment is fleeting. I will not let it define me and my future.

62. I have full trust in my intuition and wisdom. They will always guide me through these challenging times.
63. Even in this difficult time, I am choosing my peace and joy.
64. I am powerful, and I can deal with any stress that comes my way.
65. I see stressful situations as opportunities to grow into a better person.
66. I am relaxing my mind, muscles, and soul. Nothing can destroy the inner peace I have established.
67. Stress management comes naturally to me.
68. I am learning to control my stress level one step at a time.
69. I am equipped with all the things I need to overcome my stress.
70. This situation is just a moment in my beautiful life.
71. I am choosing to love and care for myself, especially during these stressful situations.
72. Today, I choose to be optimistic in every stressful situation I face.
73. I will focus my energy on the things I can control.
74. My fears are valid, but I know that worrying will not help me in my situation.
75. The stress I am feeling is understandable, but I will remain gentle with myself.

76. I can be stressed but brave in the face of great challenges.
77. I always strive to do my best, even during stressful situations.
78. I can feel overwhelmed, but I will always find a way to recover.
79. I have a healthy way of coping with stress and challenges.
80. The situation is too much for me right now, so I am taking a step back to breathe and relax.
81. I am always ready to ask for help whenever the stress is too much for me to handle.
82. I am actively looking for things to be grateful for even in these difficult times.
83. I am stressed, but I am not letting the negative thoughts penetrate my mind.
84. I am manifesting a stress-free life.
85. I am allowing myself to take deep and relaxing breaths.
86. Today, I will live life as it goes. I will not stress over things that have not happened yet.
87. I am choosing to reduce the impacts of stress on my life.
88. Today, I am introducing big and positive changes into my life.
89. I will learn how to balance the negatives and positives in my life.
90. I will constantly free myself from the burden of my stress.

91. I am a man who can remain steadfast in the face of pressure.
92. I can perform well even under stressful situations.
93. I let go of my worries and stress before I go to sleep.
94. Stress management is my specialty.
95. I have a capable mind that can withstand and recover from any type of stress life throws at me.
96. I am getting better at relieving stress.
97. There is no harm in slowing down. I solve my problems at my own pace.
98. Worrying and stressing over these matters are not fruitful. I will take deep breaths until I find my groove.
99. My positive energy can defeat all my worries.
100. I am looking forward to all the lessons I can harness from this stressful experience.
101. I am a man of color living a wonderful life.
102. My life and existence cannot please everyone, and that is okay.
103. I am a beautiful human being, and I am greater than what I think of myself.
104. I am not my depression. My life means so much more than my condition.
105. My depression is a work in progress. I know I can get over it with careful practice.

106. Everything will work out for me. It can be difficult today, but that is okay.
107. I am happy. I love myself. I love my life.
108. I love my imperfections and weaknesses. They make me human.
109. This darkness in my life is only temporary. My future is for me to decide.
110. My existence is needed by the universe. I do not have to prove this truth to anyone.
111. I am loved. I am appreciated.
112. I am so much more than my productivity, skills, and abilities. I am me.
113. I am feeling better today than yesterday.
114. I am embracing all the positive energy coming my way.
115. I am needed by the people who love me, regardless of how worthless I feel.
116. I am more powerful than my losses, fears, insecurities, and weaknesses.
117. I am a warrior. I can fight off the illness I have.
118. My mind is stronger than my depression.
119. I am a man of color deserving of love, happiness, and peace.
120. I am proud of the progress I have made.
121. I am getting better and better as the day passes.
122. My life is worth giving a chance, so I am living it in the best way possible.

123. I am learning to manage my depression one step at a time.
124. I celebrate every day that I am me.
125. I am letting go of the things that destroy me.
126. I can face all the emotions I feel because I am strong.
127. Today, I am taking another step closer to getting better.
128. I am surrounded by trustworthy and loving people who support me and my well-being.
129. The sadness I am feeling will pass because it is not truly mine.
130. I face my negative emotions with a positive attitude.
131. Being depressed is not my fault. I need not be guilty or ashamed of it.
132. I close my eyes. I take deep breaths. I know that this shall pass.
133. I love and care for myself unconditionally.
134. My life is valuable and meaningful, with or without awards.
135. My success and productivity do not define me. I mean so much more than these worldly possessions.
136. I am appreciated by my colleagues, friends, and family. I am seen and loved for who I am.
137. I celebrate every win because I deserve it.
138. I can overcome this episode and keep living this life.

139. Everything is possible as long as I keep breathing.
140. I am proud of myself for waking up and having the courage to get out of bed.
141. I take this moment to thank myself for surviving yet another day.
142. I am the captain of my ship, and I choose to feel happy, fulfilled, and at peace.
143. I can embrace all the positive emotions I have been continuously showered with.
144. I will be extra compassionate to myself.
145. I will love myself more even when it's hard.
146. I am allowing myself to do what needs to be done to cope and survive.
147. I celebrate all the hard days I surpassed and will surpass.
148. I am allowed to feel vulnerable and sensitive when I discuss my condition with another person.
149. I am patient with the progress I am making. Good things take time.
150. I am stopping myself from asking the "whys." Instead, I will focus my energy on thinking about how to get better.
151. I have people whom I can open up to and whom I can share my burdens with. The world is not for me to carry alone.
152. No matter how steep my life trails get, I know I can get through them because I am strong.

153. I am not scared of my anxiety because I can just breathe it all out.
154. I will not be held down by what could go wrong. I am excited for things to go right in my life.
155. Today, I will step out of my comfort zone because I can.
156. I will not let my negative thoughts sabotage the progress I am making.
157. Congratulations to me. I decided to get up and live another day.
158. I am patient with myself. I know that I will feel better soon.
159. This life is mine to live, and I will always try to make it worth it.
160. No one can save me but me. I am my own hero, and I'm starting my healing today.
161. I am deserving of this life, of this body, and of this soul. I refuse to believe otherwise.
162. I am proud of myself because I did what I could to survive this day.
163. I choose to understand myself more today, including my traumas, my feelings, and my issues.
164. I feel the excitement running through my veins. Today will be a great day.
165. I am letting go of my hopelessness, grief, despair, and loneliness.

166. I am my own champion who defends my peace and happiness.
167. I will not let my depression ruin the beautiful things I could have.
168. There is pride in choosing what is best for me.
169. Happiness and peace are not privileges. They are my rights, and I own them today.
170. I feel excited to wake up tomorrow with a new outlook on life.
171. I am embracing every person who offers his shoulder to me. It makes me love myself more.
172. Life is beautiful if only I am open to it.
173. Every day, I become closer to the person I have always aspired to become – free, happy, and relaxed.
174. I will not let this day stomp on my growth. I will overcome it. I prepared well for these things, and I know I can execute them properly.
175. I am having a panic attack right now, but I can definitely get better. This is only temporary. I am strong.
176. I am not afraid of committing mistakes because I know my true value.
177. It's okay that I feel sad and lonely today because this is what it takes for humans.
178. I am allowed to be imperfect.
179. My opinion of myself weighs far more significant than other people's opinions of me.

180. Life is not a race. I am allowed to live it at my own pace.
181. I will do everything I can to make the best out of this challenging and stressful situation.
182. I will not be disheartened by the setbacks I encounter along the way. They are reminders of what I can improve and do better next time.
183. I can find new things that I love. Losing one or two hobbies is not the end for me.
184. Professional help and medical help are not something I should be ashamed of. They are good for me.
185. I will spend time getting to know my condition, including the trigger. Truly, prevention is always better than cure.
186. There is no shame in seeking help. This is just another form of courage the world is yet to see.
187. I am given with the life, and I will see it to it that I live it fully.
188. I will walk until my fears and panic subside.
189. I am dedicating some time today to relaxing and doing things I love.
190. I will get through this because I always did.
191. My anxiety and depression cannot stop me from achieving greater things in life.
192. Every day I get better and better at managing and dealing with my negative thoughts.

193. I am filled with courage with every passing second.
194. There is no other version I'd rather be than the one I am now.
195. Happiness swells inside me.
196. I have the power to succeed in life regardless of the hopelessness I feel right now.
197. I fight my depression one day at a time.
198. My life is good, and I love being in it.
199. I will keep on fighting for my health and my well-being.
200. I am always hopeful that my life will get better than it is today.

www.ingramcontent.com/pod-product-compliance
Lightning Source LLC
Chambersburg PA
CBHW060527080526
44586CB00012B/655